THE INDEX-NUMBER PROBLEM
AND ITS SOLUTION

THE INDEX-NUMBER PROBLEM AND ITS SOLUTION

G. Stuvel

Emeritus Fellow of All Souls College, Oxford

MACMILLAN

First published 1989

Published by
THE MACMILLAN PRESS LTD
Houndmills, Basingstoke, Hampshire RG21 2XS
and London
Companies and representatives
throughout the world

Printed in the People's Republic of China

British Library Cataloguing in Publication Data
Stuvel, G. (Gerhard), *1917* –
The index-number problem and its solution.
1. Econometrics. Indices
I. Title
330'. 028
ISBN 0–333–49113–0

'Each maker of index-numbers is free to retain his conviction that his own plan is the very best. I only ask him to think it possible that others may not be entirely mistaken.'

(F.Y. Edgeworth in *The Economic Journal*, 1925, p. 388)

Contents

Contents

Preface

Index numbers of price and quantity such as the retail price index, the index of industrial production and the indices to be found in national accounts publications have become more and more important in the afterwar years. They affect wage negotiations, are used in econometric models that assist in forecasting and economic policy-making, and lately have begun to play a part in the index-linking of government loans, rent agreements, etc. With their growing importance it has also become increasingly important that they should be free of bias. Unfortunately, however, the index-number formulae that are most often used, those of Laspeyres and Paasche, are known to produce biased measures of price and volume change. In the old days the use of these formulae could readily be excused because the effort required to eliminate the element of bias, which was judged to be small, would have been very costly in terms of the excessive computing burden it would have entailed. But thanks to the rapid advance in computing technology that is no longer so. Thus, as the need for more appropriate indices of price and quantity is beginning to make itself felt, the possibility of filling this need at comparatively little extra cost has in many cases become a reality.

It is the object of this study to ascertain what formulae, old or new, should ideally be used in the construction of those index numbers which might eventually replace the ones in current use, bearing in mind the purposes these index numbers are designed to serve and the limitations set by data availability. The systematic search for these formulae has led me to introduce a few new ones, which in my opinion recommend themselves because of their capacity to bring the index-number problem, i.e. the problem of assigning appropriate measures of price and quantity change to commodity aggregates, as near to a solution as one could possibly hope for.

Oxford   G. STUVEL

Part I
Binary Comparisons

1 The Problem

1.1 The measurement in relative terms of the price development of a single commodity such as granulated sugar from one date to another presents no problem. Of course, we must take care that the prices at the two dates relate to the same commodity, i.e. we must make sure that to all intents and purposes the quality and the packaging have not changed and that the commodity is sold through the same type of retail outlet, etc.[1] However, once we are satisfied that indeed we are comparing like with like, all we have to do in order to express the price comparison in relative terms is to determine the ratio between the prices at the two dates. In index-number theory that ratio for a single commodity is called a price relative. When the price of commodity i at date 1, the current date, is compared with its price at date 0, the base date, the price relative, denoted by the symbol p^i, will be defined as

$$p^i = \frac{P_1^i}{P_0^i} \tag{1.1}$$

where P_1^i and P_0^i denote the prices of commodity i at dates 1 and 0 expressed in currency units per physical unit (say £s per ton). It is worth noting that p^i, unlike P_1^i and P_0^i, is quite independent of the choice of units used in the measurement of prices. Thus, for instance, if pennies are used instead of £s both P_1^i and P_0^i will be 100 times as large, but their ratio, which is p^i, will remain the same.

1.2 It is not only for single commodities that the measurement of the relative price development between two dates presents no problem. The same is true for composite commodities, i.e. collections or 'baskets' of goods and services of unchanging composition. Let there be n different goods and services in a given basket and let their quantities be denoted by Q^i ($i = 1, \ldots, n$). Then the cost or the price of that basket at date 1 will be

3

$Q^1 P_1^1 + Q^2 P_1^2 + \ldots + Q^n P_1^n = \Sigma Q^i P_1^i$, where the summation sign Σ stands for summation over i with i in this case taking the values of 1 up to n. Likewise, the cost or the price of that basket at date 0 will be $\Sigma Q^i P_0^i$. Hence the price ratio for the composite commodity when comparing date 1 with date 0, a price ratio which we shall denote by the symbol $\underline{P}$, will be

$$\underline{P} = \frac{\Sigma Q^i P_1^i}{\Sigma Q^i P_0^i} \tag{1.2}$$

Once again it is immaterial what units are used in the measurement of prices, or in the measurement of quantities for that matter. But that is not all. The size of the basket is also immaterial. Thus, for instance, if the size of the basket is increased tenfold both $\Sigma Q^i P_1^i$ and $\Sigma Q^i P_0^i$ will increase tenfold and, as a result, $\underline{P}$ will remain unaltered. However, in order for (1.2) to apply, it is necessary that the physical composition of the basket does not change from base date to current date, because if the volume structure of the collection of goods and services did change between the two dates that collection would no longer be a composite commodity.

1.3   Because of what follows it is worth noting here that $\underline{P}$, besides being the ratio of the prices of the basket at dates 1 and 0, can also be interpreted as a weighted average of the price relatives for the single commodities included in the basket and that there are actually two ways of doing this. The first way is to develop the formula for $\underline{P}$ as follows:

$$\underline{P} = \frac{\Sigma Q^i P_1^i}{\Sigma Q^i P_0^i} = \sum \frac{Q^i P_0^i}{\Sigma Q^i P_0^i} \cdot \frac{P_1^i}{P_0^i} = \Sigma \underline{w}_0^i \, p^i \tag{1.3}$$

where $\underline{w}_0^i$, the weight assigned to p^i, is the share of commodity i in the total cost of the basket at the base date. This shows $\underline{P}$ to be a base-weighted arithmetic mean of these price relatives. The other way of showing $\underline{P}$ to be a weighted average of price relatives is to develop the formula for the inverse of $\underline{P}$ as follows:

$$\frac{1}{\underline{P}} = \frac{\Sigma Q^i P_0^i}{\Sigma Q^i P_1^i} = \sum \frac{Q^i P_1^i}{\Sigma Q^i P_1^i} \cdot \frac{P_0^i}{P_1^i} = \sum \underline{w}_1^i \frac{1}{p^i} \tag{1.4}$$

where $\underline{w}_1^i$, the weight assigned to $\frac{1}{p^i}$, is the share of commodity i in the total cost of the basket at the current date. This shows $\underline{P}$ to be a current-weighted harmonic mean of the price relatives of the various goods and services that are included in the basket.

1.4 Composite commodities may be few and far between or even non-existent, but the basket approach described in sections 1.2 and 1.3 is one that is widely applied in the measurement of general price movements in the economy. Thus formula (1.3) is typical of the way in which index numbers of retail prices are calculated. The weights used in their calculation are normally base weights derived from family budget enquiries of an earlier date which price-wise but not volume-wise have been updated to the base date.

1.5 Comparisons are not always between two dates. Often it is two periods, say, two years that are being compared. In that case the prices that are being compared ought to be the average prices of the commodities involved in the two periods. For each commodity and for each period these average prices should be obtained, if possible, by dividing the value of the transactions in that commodity in that period by the quantity of that commodity transacted in that period. Then, denoting price, value and volume by the symbols P, V and Q:

$$P_0^i = V_0^i / Q_0^i \text{ and } P_1^i = V_1^i / Q_1^i \tag{1.5}$$

Where the average prices are determined in this manner and where the basket approach is followed in measuring general price developments, the data on the quantities of the commodities bought and sold in the base year and in the current year respectively can, of course, also be used as the Q^is which determine the composition of the basket in (1.2). Laspeyres (1871) was the first to use the base-year quantities in this way. The resulting price index number, which carries his name and which we shall denote by the symbol P_L, is defined as:

$$P_L = \frac{\Sigma Q_0^i P_1^i}{\Sigma Q_0^i P_0^i} \tag{1.6}$$

Its introduction was followed three years later by that of the alternative price index number which is based on a basket of current-year composition. This index number, which is due to Paasche (1874) and which is named after him, we shall denote by the symbol P_P. Its formula is

$$P_P = \frac{\Sigma Q_1^i P_1}{\Sigma Q_1^i P_0} \tag{1.7}$$

1.6 Irving Fisher (1927) defined an index number of the prices of a number of commodities as an average of their price relatives.[2] The Laspeyres and Paasche price index numbers, being of the basket type, fit this definition perfectly, as can readily be verified by substituting Q_0^i for Q^i in (1.3) and (1.4) in order to obtain the relevant expressions for P_L and by substituting Q_1^i for Q^i in (1.3) and (1.4) in order to obtain the relevant expressions for P_P. Of these four expressions, the first and the last appear to provide the most convenient definitions of the Laspeyres and the Paasche price index respectively. The former defines the Laspeyres price index as a base-weighted arithmetic mean of the price relatives of the commodities included in the index, and the latter defines the Paasche price index as a current-weighted harmonic mean of those price relatives. Thus

$$P_L = \frac{\Sigma Q_0^i P_1^i}{\Sigma Q_0^i P_0^i} = \sum \frac{Q_0^i P_0^i}{\Sigma Q_0^i P_0^i} \cdot \frac{P_1^i}{P_0^i} = \Sigma w_0^i p^i \tag{1.8}$$

and

$$\frac{1}{P_P} = \frac{\Sigma Q_1^i P_0^i}{\Sigma Q_1^i P_1^i} = \sum \frac{Q_1^i P_1^i}{\Sigma Q_1^i P_1^i} \cdot \frac{P_0^i}{P_1^i} = \sum w_1^i \frac{1}{p^i} \tag{1.9}$$

where w_0^i and w_1^i are the shares of commodity i in the total costs of the base-year and the current-year baskets respectively. As we shall see later, not all price index numbers can similarly be defined as averages of price relatives.

1.7 All that has been said so far about the measurement of relative price developments applies equally, mutatis mutandis, to the measurement of relative volume developments. Thus for a single commodity the appropriate measure will be the quantity relative, which is defined as

$$q^i = \frac{Q_1^i}{Q_0^i} \tag{1.10}$$

Given the unchanging volume structure of a composite commodity, the rate at which the quantities of the single commodities forming part of that composite commodity change from base year to current year will be the same for all of them, and this rate will also be that at which the volume of the composite commodity itself changes from base year to current year. Hence, denoting the quantity ratio for the composite commodity by the symbol $\underline{Q}$,

$$\underline{Q} = q^i \, (i = 1, \ldots, n) \tag{1.11}$$

Likewise, the price development of a collection of goods and services with an unchanging price structure will be the same as that of its parts, which all will show the same price development. Thus

$$\underline{P} = p^i \, (i = 1, \ldots, n) \tag{1.12}$$

where $\underline{P}$ denotes the price ratio from current year on base year for such a collection of goods and services with a fixed price structure. The corresponding volume development of that collection of goods and services will be measured by

$$\underline{\underline{Q}} = \frac{\Sigma P^i Q_1^i}{\Sigma P^i Q_0^i} = \Sigma \, \underline{w}_0^i \, q^i = \frac{1}{\Sigma \, \underline{w}_1^i \, \frac{1}{q^i}} \tag{1.13}$$

where $\underline{w}_0^i = P^i Q_0^i / \Sigma P^i Q_0^i$ and $\underline{w}_1^i = P^i Q_1^i / \Sigma P^i Q_1^i$

1.8 The expression for $\underline{Q}$ in (1.13) can readily be derived from the expression for $\underline{P}$ in (1.2) by replacing the Ps in the latter by Qs and vice versa without altering subscripts. By applying the same procedure of factor reversal to P_L and P_P we obtain

$$Q_L = \frac{\Sigma P_0^i Q_1^i}{\Sigma P_0^i Q_0^i} \tag{1.14}$$

and

$$Q_P = \frac{\Sigma P_1^i Q_1^i}{\Sigma P_1^i Q_0^i} \tag{1.15}$$

Like their price counterparts these volume indices are commonly referred to as Laspeyres and Paasche indices, and accordingly they are here denoted by the symbols Q_L and Q_P respectively. Not surprisingly, it turns out that these volume indices can be interpreted as weighted averages of quantity relatives in much the same way that their price counterparts could be interpreted as weighted averages of price relatives. All that is required to demonstrate this is to apply factor reversal to (1.8) and (1.9). This produces the following result:

$$Q_L = \frac{\Sigma P_0^i Q_1^i}{\Sigma P_0^i Q_0^i} = \sum \frac{P_0^i Q_0^i}{\Sigma P_0^i Q_0^i} \cdot \frac{Q_1^i}{Q_0^i} = \Sigma w_0^i q^i \qquad (1.16)$$

and

$$\frac{1}{Q_P} = \frac{\Sigma P_1^i Q_0^i}{\Sigma P_1^i Q_1^i} = \sum \frac{P_1^i Q_1^i}{\Sigma P_1^i Q_1^i} \cdot \frac{Q_0^i}{Q_1^i} = \sum w_1^i \frac{1}{q^i} \qquad (1.17)$$

1.9 Index-number makers are usually able to choose a base year which is such that the weights required for calculating a Laspeyres index number of either prices or quantities can be obtained without much difficulty. As regards the current year they have no such choice. The current year is given and frequently it will be a year for which the data needed to establish the current weights required for calculating a Paasche index number are either not available at all or are not available soon enough to be of any use. This explains why statisticians normally opt for constructing Laspeyres rather than Paasche index numbers. The indices of retail prices or the cost of living and the indices of industrial production are cases in point. The base years for the former are usually years in which family budget surveys have been carried out. These surveys provide the information needed to determine the base weights with the help of which the various price relatives can be combined into Laspeyres price index numbers. Likewise, the base years for indices of industrial production tend to be years in which a Census of Production was taken. From these censuses the required value-added weights can be derived.

1.10 When both a price index and a volume index are required to analyse the value development of a commodity aggregate from base year to current year into its price and volume components, the two indices must be such as to multiply out to the ratio of the aggregate's values in the two years compared. This means that where one of these indices is a Laspeyres index the other will be a Paasche index, because

$$\frac{\Sigma V_1^i}{\Sigma V_0^i} = \frac{\Sigma Q_1^i P_1^i}{\Sigma Q_0^i P_0^i} \equiv \frac{\Sigma Q_1^i P_0^i}{\Sigma Q_0^i P_0^i} \times \frac{\Sigma Q_1^i P_1^i}{\Sigma Q_1^i P_0^i} \equiv \frac{\Sigma Q_0^i P_1^i}{\Sigma Q_0^i P_0^i} \times \frac{\Sigma Q_1^i P_1^i}{\Sigma Q_0^i P_1^i}$$

or

$$V \equiv Q_L P_P \equiv P_L Q_P \tag{1.18}$$

where V denotes the value ratio for the aggregate. Already before the war the value development of merchandise imports and exports used to be analysed in this way, and since the war this form of analysis has spread to all important commodity aggregates recorded in the national accounts. In all these cases, the volume index is a Laspeyres index and the price index a Paasche index. There is no compelling reason why this should be so. It might easily have been the other way round. Thus, for instance, if in the immediate afterwar years the emphasis in economic policy had been on containing inflation rather than on stimulating economic growth, national accounts statisticians might well have chosen to provide data of base-year values at current-year prices ($\Sigma Q_0^i P_1^i$) rather than data of current-year values at base-year prices ($\Sigma Q_1^i P_0^i$).

1.11 Index-number makers appear to be quite content to use Laspeyres and Paasche index numbers as measures of volume and price developments of commodity aggregates which change their volume and price structures from base year to current year. Yet, strictly speaking, these index numbers are only appropriate measures of volume and price developments for commodity aggregates of which the volume structure or the price structure or both do not change from base year to current year. It is the change in these structures that causes Laspeyres and Paasche index numbers to differ from each other. To have these differing measures of price and volume developments of commodity aggregates is something which index-number theorists have been less ready to accept than index-number makers have. They have persistently searched over the last hundred years or so for measures of price and volume development which take due account of the changes in the volume and price structures of commodity aggregates from base year to current year, and which by doing so might eliminate the duality or even plurality of index-number measures. It is the problem of how this should be done which is known as the index-number problem.

1.12 The reason why index-number makers take so little notice of the index-number problem is presumably that they are under the impression that, at least for comparisons over short periods of time, it makes very little difference in practice whether one calculates an index number of either volume or price on the basis of the Laspeyres formula or on the basis of the Paasche formula, and that therefore any refinement of formula within these two extremes is no more than a matter of purely academic interest. It may well be that Irving Fisher, who made a very intensive study of index numbers, unwittingly has been responsible for creating this impression. In order to show how the choice of formula affected the numerical measure of the price and volume development of a group of commodities, he made use of statistical data on the wholesale prices and quantities marketed of thirty-six commodities for the period from 1913 to 1918.[3] These data had been collected by Wesley C. Mitchell for the War Industries Board in the United States. The price index numbers calculated by Fisher on the basis of this material, taking 1913 as the base year and 1918 as the current year, were $P_L = 1.7787$ and $P_P = 1.7743$. Thus the two measures appeared to be almost the same.

1.13 Some fifty years after Fisher carried out his calculations on the US War Industries Board material, R.F. Fowler (1970) used the basic data from which the UK Index of retail prices is calculated to make a comparison between the Laspeyres and the Paasche measures of price change for the period from 1958 to 1967. His main finding was that the all-items retail price index for the United Kingdom increased from 1958 to 1967 by 29.45 per cent if calculated on the basis of the Laspeyres formula and by 23.40 per cent if calculated on the basis of the Paasche formula.[4] Clearly, where the two formulae can produce results that differ so widely, the solving of the index-number problem becomes a matter of more than purely academic interest, particularly in view of the important part played by index numbers of price and quantity in wage bargaining and in the design and conduct of government economic policy.

1.14 The gaps between the Paasche and the Laspeyres index numbers of quantity and price, i.e. $(Q_P - Q_L)$ and $(P_P - P_L)$, can be either positive or negative and sometimes will be large and sometimes will be small or even non-existent. What accounts for these differences in sign and size can be seen from the following breakdown of the relative gap between Paasche and Laspeyres indices, or gap coefficient (g) as we shall call it, into its component parts (see also the note on p. 107).

$$g = \frac{Q_P - Q_L}{Q_L} = \frac{P_P - P_L}{P_L} = r_{w_0}(q, p) \cdot \frac{s_{w_0}(q)}{Q_L} \cdot \frac{s_{w_0}(p)}{P_L} \quad (1.19)$$

where

$$r_{w_0}(q, p) = \frac{\text{Cov}_{w_0}(q, p)}{s_{w_0}(q)s_{w_0}(p)}$$

and where

$$\text{Cov}_{w_0}(q, p) = \Sigma w_0^i (q^i - Q_L)(p^i - P_L) = V - Q_L P_L$$

$$s_{w_0}(q) = \sqrt{\Sigma w_0^i (q^i - Q_L)^2}$$

$$s_{w_0}(p) = \sqrt{\Sigma w_0^i (p^i - P_L)^2}$$

This three-way breakdown of the gap coefficient was introduced into index-number theory by von Bortkiewicz (1923).

1.15 What (1.19) shows is that the size and sign of the gap coefficient depends on

(1) $r_{w_0}(q, p)$ = the base-weighted coefficient of correlation between the quantity and the price relatives,

(2) $\dfrac{s_{w_0}(q)}{Q_L}$ = the base-weighted relative standard deviation, or coefficient of variation, of the quantity relatives,

(3) $\dfrac{s_{w_0}(p)}{P_L}$ = the base-weighted relative standard deviation, or coefficient of variation, of the quantity relatives,

Where any of these three multiplicative components of the gap coefficient is zero, the gap coefficient itself will be zero. Thus there will be no gap between the Paasche and Laspeyres indices of either quantity or price

(i) if the quantity and price relatives are completely uncorrelated, or

(ii) if there is no spread among the quantity relatives, i.e. if they are all the same, or

(iii) if there is no spread among the price relatives, i.e. if they are all the same.

In all other cases, there will be a gap and it will be the larger (smaller) the stronger (weaker) the correlation between the quantity and the price relatives is and the larger (smaller) the relative spread of each set of these relatives is. The absolute gap is, of course, also affected by the value of the index concerned, because

$$Q_P - Q_L = Q_L \times g \tag{1.20}$$

and

$$P_P - P_L = P_L \times g \tag{1.21}$$

Finally, the sign of the gap will depend on whether the correlation between the quantity and the price relatives is positive or negative. If it is positive the value of the Paasche indices will exceed that of the Laspeyres indices and if it is negative the reverse will hold.[5]

2 The Traditional Approach

2.1 The traditional way of dealing with the index-number problem has been to design measures based on some sort of averaging process, aimed at breaking away from the obvious one-sidedness of the Laspeyres and the Paasche measures. In its simplest form this approach to the problem, if applied to the measurement of the price development of a commodity aggregate, leads one to suggest that maybe this development can best be measured by the arithmetic mean of the Laspeyres and the Paasche price index:

$$P(AM) = \frac{P_L + P_P}{2} \tag{2.1}$$

However, apart from its simplicity, there is no reason why the arithmetic mean should be preferred to the harmonic mean:

$$P(HM) = \frac{2}{\dfrac{1}{P_L} + \dfrac{1}{P_P}} = \frac{2 P_L P_P}{P_P + P_L} \tag{2.2}$$

or to the geometric mean

$$P(GM) = \sqrt{P_L P_P} \tag{2.3}$$

Indeed, if one has to choose between these three types of average, one might well prefer the geometric mean to the other two, since the geometric mean is itself a mean of the other two:

$$P(GM) = \sqrt{P(AM)P(HM)} \tag{2.4}$$

13

But that is not all. Irving Fisher, after examining well over a hundred possible index-number formulae, reached the conclusion that $P(GM)$ was in fact the 'ideal' index number (see the note on p. 99). Because of Fisher's advocacy of this particular index-number form, it has become known as the Fisher price index. In accordance with this, we shall denote it henceforth by the symbol P_F. Thus

$$P_F = \sqrt{P_L P_P} \tag{2.5}$$

2.2 Attempts at taking account of changes in the composition of a commodity aggregate from base year to current year when calculating the measure of its relative price development between those two years have not been confined to taking some form of average of P_L and P_P. Another suggested solution of the index-number problem has been to base the calculation of that measure not on either the base-year basket (as in P_L) or the current-year basket (as in P_P) but on the average of the two. This solution was first proposed in Edgeworth (1888).[1] The index resulting from this approach to the problem, which we shall denote by the symbol P_E, is the following:

$$P_E = \frac{\Sigma(Q_0^i + Q_1^i)P_1^i}{\Sigma(Q_0^i + Q_1^i)P_0^i} = \frac{P_L + V}{1 + Q_L} = \frac{1 + Q_P}{1 + Q_L}\, P_L \tag{2.6}$$

2.3 It should be noted that the Edgeworth price index (P_E) is based on an average of two baskets that generally will not be equal in size. This difference in size can be corrected for by dividing the Q_1^is in the formula for P_E by either Q_L or Q_P. The new indices thus obtained may be said to be based on an average of the volume structures of the aggregate in the base year and the current year respectively. Interestingly, these two indices turn out to be $P(AM)$ and $P(HM)$ because

$$\frac{\Sigma\left(Q_0^i + \dfrac{Q_1^i}{Q_L}\right)P_1^i}{\Sigma\left(Q_0^i + \dfrac{Q_1^i}{Q_L}\right)P_0^i} = \frac{\Sigma Q_0^i P_1^i + \dfrac{1}{Q_L}\Sigma Q_1^i P_1^i}{\Sigma Q_0^i P_0^i + \dfrac{1}{Q_L}\Sigma Q_1^i P_0^i} = \frac{P_L + \dfrac{V}{Q_L}}{1 + 1}$$

$$= \frac{P_L + P_P}{2} = P(AM)$$

and

$$\frac{\sum\left(Q_0^i + \dfrac{Q_1^i}{Q_P}\right)P_1^i}{\sum\left(Q_0^i + \dfrac{Q_1^i}{Q_P}\right)P_0^i} = \frac{Q_P\Sigma Q_0^i P_1^i + \Sigma Q_1^i P_1^i}{Q_P\Sigma Q_0^i P_0^i + \Sigma Q_1^i P_0^i} = \frac{Q_P P_L + V}{Q_P + Q_L}$$

$$= \frac{2V}{Q_P + Q_L} = \frac{2}{\dfrac{1}{P_L} + \dfrac{1}{P_P}} = P(HM)$$

Thus we find that $P(AM)$ and $P(HM)$ are not only the arithmetic and harmonic means of the Laspeyres and Paasche price indices but equally price indices based on average volume structures.

2.4 It is always possible to derive from a given price index number a corresponding volume index number by means of factor reversal (see section 1.8). Thus we find that the following volume index numbers correspond to the price index numbers defined in (2.1)–(2.6):

$$Q(AM) = \frac{Q_L + Q_P}{2} \tag{2.7}$$

$$Q(HM) = \frac{2}{\dfrac{1}{Q_L} + \dfrac{1}{Q_P}} = \frac{2Q_L Q_P}{Q_P + Q_L} \tag{2.8}$$

$$Q(GM) = \sqrt{Q_L Q_P} \tag{2.9}$$

$$Q(GM) = \sqrt{Q(AM)Q(HM)} \tag{2.10}$$

$$Q_F = \sqrt{Q_L Q_P} \tag{2.11}$$

and

$$Q_E = \frac{\Sigma(P_0^i + P_1^i)Q_1^i}{\Sigma(P_0^i + P_1^i)Q_0^i} = \frac{Q_L + V}{1 + P_L} = \frac{1 + P_P}{1 + P_L}Q_L \tag{2.12}$$

Incidentally, the last of these index numbers cannot be attributed to Edgeworth. It simply owes the symbol Q_E to the fact that it has been derived from P_E by factor reversal in much the same way that Q_L and Q_P were derived from P_L and P_P. Another point worth noting is that $Q(AM)$ and $Q(HM)$ can be shown to be volume indices based on average price structures in the same way that, in section 2.3, $P(AM)$ and $P(HM)$ were shown to be price indices based on average volume structures.

2.5 In section 1.10 we saw how the value development of a commodity aggregate from base year to current year can be analysed into a price and a volume component with the help of a Laspeyres price index and a Paasche volume index, or alternatively with a Paasche price index and a Laspeyres volume index. A similar analysis can also be carried out with the hybrid indices which are discussed in this chapter, for it turns out that

$$V \equiv P(AM)Q(HM) \equiv P(HM)Q(AM) \equiv P_F Q_F \qquad (2.13)$$

because

$$\frac{P_L + P_P}{2} \times \frac{2}{\dfrac{1}{Q_L} + \dfrac{1}{Q_P}} = \frac{(P_L + P_P)Q_L Q_P}{Q_P + Q_L} = \frac{VQ_L + VQ_P}{Q_L + Q_P} = V$$

$$\frac{2}{\dfrac{1}{P_L} + \dfrac{1}{P_P}} \times \frac{Q_L + Q_P}{2} = \frac{P_L P_P(Q_L + Q_P)}{P_P + P_L} = \frac{VP_L + VP_P}{P_L + P_P} = V$$

and

$$P_F Q_F = \sqrt{P_L P_P} \times \sqrt{Q_L Q_P} = \sqrt{P_L P_P Q_L Q_P} = \sqrt{V \cdot V} = V$$

2.6 The index-number pairs in (1.18) and (2.13) are by no means the only pairs of index numbers multiplying out to the value ratio (V). Actually, for each price index number we can conceive of a volume index number such that the two multiply out to the value ratio. Thus, for instance, the volume index which forms such a pair with the Edgeworth price index is

$$\frac{V}{P_E} = \frac{1+Q_L}{1+Q_P} Q_P \tag{2.14}$$

Likewise, we find that the price index which with the volume index Q_E multiplies out to the value ratio is

$$\frac{V}{Q_E} = \frac{1+P_L}{1+P_P} P_P \tag{2.15}$$

2.7 For pairs of index numbers to multiply out to the value ratio is clearly not so unusual. However, for the members of such a pair to be such that the one can be obtained from the other by factor reversal is less common, although by no means unique. Of the pairs shown in (1.18) and (2.13) the pair of Fisher index numbers (P_F, Q_F) is the only pair of which the numbers can be obtained from each other by factor reversal. However, it should be realised that there exists a general procedure for constructing such pairs. This procedure, which is due to Irving Fisher,[2] consists of the following steps. Let the particular index number with which we start be a price index (P). Then the first thing to do is to apply factor reversal so as to ascertain which volume index (Q) corresponds to it. Next we must find out which is the price index which with this volume index will multiply out to the value ratio. This index (V/Q) is called the factor antithesis of the original price index (P). By taking the geometric mean of the original price index (P) and its factor antithesis (V/Q), we then obtain a price index which when multiplied with a volume index derived from it by factor reversal will yield the value ratio. Thus

$$V \equiv \left(P\frac{V}{Q}\right)^{1/2}\left(Q\frac{V}{P}\right)^{1/2} \tag{2.16}$$

For $P = P_L$ this works out at

$$V \equiv \left(P_L\frac{V}{Q_L}\right)^{1/2}\left(Q_L\frac{V}{P_L}\right)^{1/2} = (P_L P_P)^{1/2}(Q_L Q_P)^{1/2} = P_F Q_F \tag{2.17}$$

Not surprisingly the same result is obtained for $P = P_P$, because

$$V \equiv \left(P_P\frac{V}{Q_P}\right)^{1/2}\left(Q_P\frac{V}{P_P}\right)^{1/2} = (P_P P_L)^{1/2}(Q_P Q_L)^{1/2} = P_F Q_F \tag{2.18}$$

With the help of (2.4) and (2.13) it can be shown in much the same way that for $P = P(AM)$ and for $P = P(HM)$ we also end up with the Fisher index-number pair, because

$$V = \left(P(AM)\frac{V}{Q(AM)}\right)^{1/2}\left(Q(AM)\frac{V}{P(AM)}\right)^{1/2}$$
$$= (P_L P_P)^{1/2}(Q_L Q_P)^{1/2} = P_F Q_F \tag{2.19}$$

and

$$V = \left(P(HM)\frac{V}{Q(HM)}\right)^{1/2}\left(Q(HM)\frac{V}{P(HM)}\right)^{1/2}$$
$$= (P_L P_P)^{1/2}(Q_L Q_P)^{1/2} = P_F Q_F \tag{2.20}$$

However, this does not mean that the procedure described above and embodied in (2.16) will always lead to the Fisher index-number pair, no matter what its starting point is. Thus, for instance, for $P = P_E$

$$V \equiv \left(P_E \frac{V}{Q_E}\right)^{1/2}\left(Q_E \frac{V}{P_E}\right)^{1/2} = (e^{1/2} P_F)(e^{1/2} Q_F) \tag{2.21}$$

where

$$e = \frac{1 + P_L + Q_P + V}{1 + Q_L + P_P + V}$$

as can be verified quite easily with the help of the expressions for P_E and $\frac{V}{Q_E}$ in (2.6) and (2.15) respectively.

2.8   The six hybrid price index numbers introduced in this chapter normally do not differ much numerically. In Fisher's example (see section 1.12), the differences between them are in fact so small as to be almost non-existent, but then, of course, the Laspeyres and Paasche indices in that example had numerical values that were extraordinarily close to each other to start with. In other examples, where the differences between the values of the Laspeyres and Paasche price indices are considerable, the differences between the values of these hybrid price indices still tend to be comparatively small, as can be seen from Table 2.1 below which has been calculated on the basis of information provided in Fowler's study (see section 1.13).

TABLE 2.1   Various indices of UK retail prices for 1967 (1958 = 100)

	All items	Food	Transport and vehicles
P_L	129.45	122.80	131.31
P_P	123.40	120.82	103.28
P_F	126.39	121.81	116.45
$P(AM)$	126.43	121.81	117.29
$P(HM)$	126.35	121.80	115.62
P_E	126.09	121.78	111.47
$\left(P_E \dfrac{V}{Q_E}\right)^{\frac{1}{2}}$	126.42	121.84	114.45
V/Q_E	126.74	121.90	117.52

The table also shows a clear tendency for the differences between the
various hybrid indices to increase as the gap between the Laspeyres
and Paasche indices widens. However, even for the Transport and
Vehicles Group for which the difference between P_L and P_P is
exceptionally large, the differences between the hybrid indices, with
the exception of P_E, are still rather small. That the numerical values
of these hybrid indices are found to differ so little is, of course, no
reason for judging them to be the best measures conceivable for the
price development of commodity aggregates. In fact all that these
findings show us is that it does not make very much difference which
particular averaging process is adopted in attempts to solve the
index-number problem, be it by way of averaging either the Laspeyres and Paasche indices themselves or the price and volume structures or the commodity baskets on which they are based.

2.9   All hybrid indices we have come across in this chapter can be
expressed in terms of the value ratio (V) and the Laspeyres indices of
volume and price (Q_L and P_L). The Paasche indices P_P and Q_P which
also appear in the formulae for these hybrid indices are, of course,
readily obtainable from V, Q_L and P_L by (1.18). Unfortunately,
national accounts statistics, even when providing us with all the
information needed to calculate V and Q_L for the various commodity
flows, normally do not enable us to calculate P_L for these flows. The
$\Sigma Q_0^i P_0^i$ and $\Sigma Q_1^i P_1^i$ data required to determine the value ratios (V)
from year 1 on year 0 for private and public consumption, capital
formation, imports and exports can be obtained from a table providing the current values of these commodity aggregates for a series of

years including years 0 and 1. Likewise, the $\Sigma Q_1^i P_0^i$ data, which together with the $\Sigma Q_0^i P_0^i$ data are required to determine the Laspeyres volume indices (Q_L) for these commodity flows, can be obtained from a table providing the deflated values of these flows if those deflated values are expressed in the prices of year 0. What is virtually always missing is a table providing information on what might be called the inflated values of these flows, i.e. information on the sum of the base-year quantities of the component elements of these flows (i.e. single commodities) valued at current-year prices ($\Sigma Q_0^i P_1^i$). It is the absence of that information which prevents the calculation of Laspeyres price indices (P_L) for these flows.

2.10 The provision of $\Sigma Q_0^i P_1^i$ data should not present national accounts statisticians with any problems, because whenever they are able to deflate a current value $V_1^i = Q_1^i P_1^i$, to $Q_1^i P_0^i$ they ought to be able to use the same price relative (P_1^i / P_0^i), which they use for that purpose, to inflate the corresponding base-year value $V_0^i = Q_0^i P_0^i$ to $Q_0^i P_1^i$. By not providing these $\Sigma Q_0^i P_1^i$ data national accounts statisticians oblige the users of their statistics to rely on Laspeyres volume indices and Paasche price indices for the measurement of the volume and price developments of the various commodity flows recorded in the accounts. This, in my view, is rather regrettable, because we know that Q_L and P_P are indices which are not fully appropriate to the measurement of the volume and price developments of aggregates of which the volume and price structures change from base year to current year (see section 1.11). As a matter of fact, the Q_L, P_P pair of indices cannot claim to be superior in any way to the alternative Q_P, P_L pair. Of course, if these alternative measures of volume development (Q_L and Q_P) and of price development (P_L and P_P) were always very close to each other numerically, this would not be a matter of much importance. However, we do know now (see section 1.13) that even for short-term comparisons they can differ considerably. The possibility of this happening argues strongly in favour of providing the $\Sigma Q_0^i P_1^i$ data, because not only would this allow the user of the statistics to decide for himself which type of index to employ for the measurement of the price development and the volume development of the various commodity aggregates, but it would also enable him to assess the degree of uncertainty that attaches to these measures.

3 The Analytical Approach

3.1 The traditional approach to the index-number problem, which we discussed in Chapter 2, has produced quite a variety of average measures of price and volume developments of commodity aggregates, which are positioned in between the Laspeyres and Paasche measures. Normally they do not differ much numerically, particularly in short-term comparisons. This makes the choice between these different average measures a matter of little consequence in those cases where what is needed is no more than a measure of price development on its own or a measure of volume development on its own. All the same, a choice will have to be made and, apart from such considerations as simplicity of formula, speed of calculation and the like, that choice is likely to be determined by a comparison of the properties which the various hybrid index numbers possess. The testing of index numbers to find out which properties they do and which properties they do not have is discussed in Chapter 4.

3.2 Where, as in national accounts analysis, index numbers of price and quantity have to be used in conjunction with each other, the question which properties different types of index number possess becomes a matter of prime importance, because much of the usefulness of those index numbers in analysis will depend on it. Actually the importance of the index numbers having the right properties for analysis is so great that it becomes advisable to reverse the order of things, by specifying first what properties are essential for the purposes of analysis and then to find out what index numbers can be devised that possess these properties. It is this analytical approach to the index-number problem which we shall deal with in the present chapter.

3.3 The values of the total purchases or sales or accumulation of a single commodity, or of a group of commodities, in the current year and in the base year respectively can be related to each other not only

21

by their ratio but also by their difference. Each such value ratio and each such value difference can be analysed into a quantity and a price component. In the case of ratios, the form of this analysis will be multiplicative (as it was shown to be in sections 1.10 and 2.5–2.7) and in the case of differences it will be additive.

3.4   Starting with the multiplicative analysis of the value ratio from the current year on the base year for a single commodity into a volume and a price component, we note that it takes the form of an identity

$$v^i \equiv q^i p^i \tag{3.1}$$

where $v^i = V_1^i / V_0^i$ = value ratio
$q^i = Q_1^i / Q_0^i$ = quantity relative
$p^i = P_1^i / P_0^i$ = price relative.

That this particular analysis should take the form of an identity is due to the fact that not only the value ratio but also the quantity and price relatives are uniquely determined as ratios between current-year and base-year magnitudes, and to the fact that prices are defined in such a way (cf. section 1.5) that in both years the value is identically equal to the product of volume and price.

3.5   Matters are different with respect to the comparable analysis for commodity aggregates which takes the form

$$V = QP \tag{3.2}$$

where V = value ratio
Q = volume index
P = price index.

Here the value ratio is still uniquely determined, but the volume and price indices are not. Consequently, the numerical values of the volume and the price component of the value change will depend on what indices are chosen for their measurement. The only limitation in their choice is that they must be such that they multiply out to the value ratio. Not all index-number pairs satisfy this condition. Thus, for instance, $V \neq Q_L P_L$ and also $V \neq Q_P P_P$. However, there are also plenty of index-number pairs which satisfy the condition laid down in

(3.2). As a matter of fact we already encountered some of them earlier on (see sections 1.10 and 2.5–2.7). The best known of these are the Q_L, P_P, the Q_P, P_L and the Q_F, P_F pairs. But there are many, many more such pairs than the few we have dealt with so far, because for every conceivable Q there is a $P(=V/Q)$ which will satisfy the condition $V = QP$ and for every conceivable P there is likewise a $Q(= V/P)$ which will satisfy that condition. One could even argue that the number of index-number pairs satisfying the condition $V = QP$ is unlimited, because there are whole classes of them each of which embraces an infinite number of such pairs. Thus, for instance, the Q_L, P_P and the Q_P, P_L pairs belong to the class in which the $Q = Q_L^\alpha Q_P^{1-\alpha}$ and the corresponding $P = P_P^\alpha P_L^{1-\alpha}$ and where α is a free parameter such that $1 \geqslant \alpha \geqslant 0$. The Q_L, P_P pair is the member of this class for which $\alpha = 1$ and the Q_P, P_L pair is the member for which $\alpha = 0$. The best known other member of this class is the Q_F, P_F pair which is obtained for $\alpha = \frac{1}{2}$.

3.6 Turning now to the additive analysis of value differences, the first thing to note is that even for single commodities this type of analysis is not uniquely determined, since there are different ways in which the volume and the price component can be separated from each other. If the base-year quantity at the current-year price is used as a means of separating them, then the additive analysis of the absolute change in value between base year and current year for a single commodity will take the form

$$V_1^i - V_0^i = (Q_1^i P_1^i - Q_0^i P_1^i) + (Q_0^i P_1^i - Q_0^i P_0^i) \tag{3.3}$$

where the quantity component measures the difference in quantity $(Q_1^i - Q_0^i)$ at the current-year price (P_1^i), while the price component measures the difference in price $(P_1^i - P_0^i)$ for the base-year quantity (Q_0^i). If, on the other hand, the current-year quantity at the base-year price is used to separate the absolute change in value into its two components, the analysis will take the form

$$V_1^i - V_0^i = (Q_1^i P_0^i - Q_0^i P_0^i) + (Q_1^i P_1^i - Q_1^i P_0^i) \tag{3.4}$$

where the quantity component measures the difference in quantity $(Q_1^i - Q_0^i)$ at the base-year price (P_0^i) and the price component measures the difference in price $(P_1^i - P_0^i)$ for the current-year quantity (Q_1^i).

3.7 The difference between the current-year value and the base-year value of a commodity aggregate is equal to the sum of the corresponding value differences of the single commodities that form part of the aggregate. Consistency between the whole and its parts likewise requires that the quantity component of the value change of a commodity aggregate from base year to current year is equal to the sum of the corresponding quantity components of the value changes of the single commodities included in the aggregate. Mutatis mutandis, the same consistency requirement applies to the price components of the value changes of the aggregate and its parts. Bearing in mind that sums of differences are equal to differences of sums and may be presented as such, the two alternative forms of additive analysis of the absolute value change of a commodity aggregate from base year to current year into a quantity and a price component may be presented as

$$\Sigma V_1^i - \Sigma V_0^i = (\Sigma Q_1^i P_1^i - \Sigma Q_0^i P_1^i) + (\Sigma Q_0^i P_1^i - \Sigma Q_0^i P_0^i) \qquad (3.5)$$

and

$$\Sigma V_1^i - \Sigma V_0^i = (\Sigma Q_1^i P_0^i - \Sigma Q_0^i P_0^i) + (\Sigma Q_1^i P_1^i - \Sigma Q_1^i P_0^i) \qquad (3.6)$$

respectively.

3.8 So far attention has been concentrated on the additive analysis of absolute changes in value from base year to current year. It is, of course, equally possible to apply this type of analysis to relative changes in value. All that is required to do so is to divide formulae (3.3)–(3.6) on both sides by the base-year value concerned, which in the case of single commodities is $V_0^i = Q_0^i P_0^i$ and in the case of commodity aggregates $\Sigma V_0^i = \Sigma Q_0^i P_0^i$. The resulting formulae for the additive analysis of relative changes in value are:

for single commodities –

$$v^i - 1 = (v^i - p^i) + (p^i - 1) = p^i(q^i - 1) + (p^i - 1) \qquad (3.7)$$

and

$$v^i - 1 = (q^i - 1) + (v^i - q^i) = (q^i - 1) + q^i(p^i - 1) \qquad (3.8)$$

for commodity aggregates –

$$V - 1 = (V - P_L) + (P_L - 1) = P_L(Q_P - 1) + (P_L - 1) \quad (3.9)$$

and

$$V - 1 = (Q_L - 1) + (V - Q_L) = (Q_L - 1) + Q_L(P_P - 1)$$
$$(3.10)$$

3.9 Formulae (3.7) to (3.10) bring out quite clearly the one-sidedness of each of the two alternative forms of additive analysis. Thus, for instance, in (3.7) the price component of the relative change in value is represented by the relative change in price $\left[p^i - 1 = \dfrac{P_1^i - P_0^i}{P_0^i} \right]$, but the quantity component is represented by the relative change in quantity $\left[q^i - 1 = \dfrac{Q_1^i - Q_0^i}{Q_0^i} \right]$ times the price relative $\left[p^i = \dfrac{P_1^i}{P_0^i} \right]$. On the other hand, in (3.8) it is the quantity

component which appears simply as $(q^i - 1)$ and the price component which appears as $(p^i - 1)$ multiplied by q^i. When $p^i > 1$ and $q^i > 1$ this will result in (3.7), as compared with (3.8), assigning a larger share to the quantity component and a correspondingly smaller share to the price component in the additive analysis of the relative change in value from base year to current year for a single commodity. The same is true, of course, with respect to the additive analysis of the corresponding absolute change in value. Also, one can make similar observations with respect to the additive analysis of the change in the value of commodity aggregates from base year to current year. However, it should be noted that in the case of commodity aggregates the comparison between the two alternative forms of additive analysis is slightly more complicated due to the fact that the relative change in quantity is measured by $(Q_P - 1)$ in (3.9) and by $(Q_L - 1)$ in (3.10), while conversely the relative change in price is measured by $(P_L - 1)$ in (3.9) and by $(P_P - 1)$ in (3.10). None the less, the fact remains that, even in the case of commodity aggregates, the two alternative forms of analysis outlined above each appear to be distinctly one-sided in opposite directions, with (3.9) attributing $[(V + 1) - (P_L + Q_L)]$ more to the quantity component and less to the price component of the value change than (3.10).

3.10 The two alternative forms of additive analysis of value changes, which were discussed in the preceding four sections, are not the only ones that guarantee the preservation of consistency between the whole and the parts when applied to commodity aggregates and to the single commodities which form part of these aggregates. Any weighted average of the two will equally preserve that consistency. Assigning weights of w and $(1 - w)$ respectively to the first and the second of these two alternative forms of additive analysis, we obtain the following generalised form of additive analysis of relative value changes:

for single commodities –

$$\begin{aligned}
v^i - 1 &= [w(v^i - p^i) + (1 - w)(q^i - 1)] + \\
&\quad + [w(p^i - 1) + (1 - w)(v^i - q^i)] \\
&= [wp^i + (1 - w)](q^i - 1) + [w + (1 - w)q^i](p^i - 1)
\end{aligned} \tag{3.11}$$

for commodity aggregates –

$$\begin{aligned}
V - 1 &= [w(V - P_L) + (1 - w)(Q_L - 1)] + \\
&\quad + [w(P_L - 1) + (1 - w)(V - Q_L)] \\
&= [wP_L(Q_P - 1) + (1 - w)(Q_L - 1)] + \\
&\quad + [w(P_L - 1) + (1 - w)Q_L(P_P - 1)]
\end{aligned} \tag{3.12}$$

where w is a constant such that $1 \geqslant w \geqslant 0$.

It should be noted once again that the correspondence between the additive analysis for single commodities on the one hand and commodity aggregates on the other, although close, is not perfect. This is exemplified by the second formulation of (3.12) as compared with the second formulation of (3.11), the point being that in the former two different measures of volume change and two different measures of price change appear as against only one measure for each in the latter.

3.11 Obviously the simplest device to prevent the additive analysis of value changes from being biased in either one direction or the other is to put $w = \frac{1}{2}$. This is equivalent to using a straight average or unweighted mean of the two alternative forms of additive analysis introduced earlier. Upon putting $w = \frac{1}{2}$, (3.11) and (3.12) reduce to

$$v^i - 1 = \tfrac{1}{2}(v^i - p^i + q^i - 1) + \tfrac{1}{2}(v^i - q^i + p^i - 1) \qquad (3.13)$$

$$= \frac{p^i + 1}{2}(q^i - 1) + \frac{q^i + 1}{2}(p^i - 1)$$

and

$$V - 1 = \tfrac{1}{2}(V - P_L + Q_L - 1) + \tfrac{1}{2}(V - Q_L + P_L - 1) \qquad (3.14)$$

$$= \tfrac{1}{2}[P_L(Q_P - 1) + (Q_L - 1)] + \tfrac{1}{2}[Q_L(P_P - 1) + (P_L - 1)]$$

respectively. Essentially this procedure, designed to avoid bias in the additive analysis of value changes into a quantity and a price component, amounts to the following. In analysing absolute changes the quantity component is established by valuing the quantity change of each single commodity from the base year to the current year, not at the base-year price or the current-year price but at the average of the two. Likewise, the price component is established by relating the price change of each single commodity to the average of its base-year and its current-year quantity. Thus

$$V_1^i - V_0^i = \frac{P_1^i + P_0^i}{2}\left(Q_1^i - Q_0^i\right) + \frac{Q_1^i + Q_0^i}{2}\left(P_1^i - P_0^i\right)$$

$$= \tfrac{1}{2}(Q_1^i P_1^i - Q_0^i P_1^i + Q_1^i P_0^i - Q_0^i P_0^i)$$

$$+ \tfrac{1}{2}(Q_1^i P_1^i - Q_1^i P_0^i + Q_0^i P_1^i - Q_0^i P_0^i)$$

a formula which upon division of both sides by $V_0^i = Q_0^i P_0^i$ turns into (3.13). In passing, it may be noted that this procedure bears some resemblance, albeit a rather superficial one, to the procedure on which the construction of the Edgeworth price index is based.

3.12 Not only does (3.12) point the way on how to avoid bias in the additive analysis of value changes, it also shows us what condition an index-number pair has to satisfy in order to ensure that consistency will be preserved between the analysis for the whole and that for the parts. Rewriting the first formulation of (3.12) as follows

$$V - 1 = [\{wV - (1 - w)\} - \{wP_L - (1 - w)Q_L\}] + \qquad (3.15)$$

$$+ [\{(1 - w)V - w\} + \{wP_L - (1 - w)Q_L\}]$$

we note that the P_L and Q_L terms appear in the same combination, namely $\{wP_L - (1 - w)Q_L\}$, in both the quantity component and the price component, in the one with a negative and in the other with a positive sign. Hence any index-number pair Q, P, which satisfies the condition

$$wP - (1 - w)Q = wP_L - (1 - w)Q_L \tag{3.16}$$

will ensure consistency between the whole and the parts in an additive analysis of value changes of commodity aggregates between base year and current year into a quantity and a price component. A more concise formulation of that condition is

$$\frac{P - P_L}{Q - Q_L} = c \tag{3.17}$$

where $c\left(= \dfrac{1 - w}{w}\right)$ is a non-negative constant. The equivalence of (3.16) and (3.17) can readily be verified by rewriting the former as $w(P - P_L) = (1 - w)(Q - Q_L)$.

3.13 For $w = 1$ (3.16) reduces to $P = P_L$ and that means that the choice of Q is left entirely free. That is as it should be, because $w = 1$ takes us back to the first of the two alternative forms of additive analysis which we considered at the outset and, as the first formulation of that alternative in (3.9) shows, the only requirement for that analysis to be consistent with the corresponding analysis of its parts, as set out in (3.7), is indeed that $P = P_L$; with respect to V there is of course no choice, since V is uniquely determined. It is only when the condition for multiplicative analysis ($V = QP$) is also brought to bear on the choice of index-number pair – as it has to be in the second formulation of (3.9) – that one cannot choose Q freely any longer. Then – given $P = P_L$ – it must be $Q = Q_P$. Just as (3.16) reduces to $P = P_L$ for $w = 1$, it reduces to $Q = Q_L$ for $w = 0$ and that leaves the choice of P entirely free. This is confirmed by the first formulation given in (3.10) to the second of the two alternative forms of additive analysis referred to above. Introduction of the condition for multiplicative analysis results in this case in $P = P_P$ as is evident from the second formulation of (3.10) where V had to be decomposed into a Q and a P. The index-number pair Q_L,P_P is the one that is conventionally used in national accounting. Hence the customary type of additive analysis there is the type described in (3.10).

3.14 Of course, the index-number pairs Q_P, P_L (for $w = 1$) and Q_L, P_P (for $w = 0$) are by no means the only ones that simultaneously satisfy the condition for multiplicative analysis and the condition for consistency between the whole and the parts in additive analysis. There is in fact one such a pair for every conceivable value of w. The general formulae for the volume and price index numbers in all these pairs for which $0 < w < 1$ can readily be derived from (3.2) and (3.16), which are the formulae expressing the two conditions these index numbers have to satisfy. Developing first the formula for Q, we find that – since according to (3.2) $V = QP$ – we can substitute V/Q for P in (3.16) and that the result of this is

$$wV/Q - (1 - w)Q = wP_L - (1 - w)Q_L$$

Upon multiplication of both sides of this equation by Q the following quadratic equation in Q is obtained:

$$wV - (1 - w)Q^2 = [wP_L - (1 - w)Q_L]Q$$

After dividing both sides by $(1 - w)$ and rearranging this becomes

$$Q^2 - \left[Q_L - \frac{w}{1 - w}P_L \right] Q - \frac{w}{1 - w}V = 0$$

By solving this equation towards its unknown, Q, we find that

$$Q = \frac{1}{2}\left[\left(Q_L - \frac{w}{1 - w}P_L \right) + \right.$$

$$\left. + \sqrt{\left(Q_L - \frac{w}{1 - w}P_L \right)^2 + 4\frac{w}{1 - w}V} \right] \qquad (3.18)$$

The other root of the quadratic equation, i.e. the one in which the square-root sign is preceded by a minus instead of a plus sign, must be rejected as being meaningless since, given that $V \geq 0$, it would result in $Q \leq 0$. Just as the general formula for Q was obtained by substituting V/Q for P in (3.16), one can obtain the general formula for P by substituting V/P for Q in (3.16). Alternatively, one can obtain that formula by substituting for Q in (3.16) the expression for Q given in (3.18). Either way the result will be

$$P = \frac{1}{2} \left[\left(P_L - \frac{1-w}{w} Q_L \right) + \right.$$

$$\left. + \sqrt{ \left(P_L - \frac{1-w}{w} Q_L \right)^2 + 4 \frac{1-w}{w} V } \right] \tag{3.19}$$

3.15 With the help of (3.16) and (3.2), which formulate the compatibility conditions[1] for index-number pairs in additive and multiplicative analysis of value changes of commodity aggregates from base year to current year into a volume and a price component, we can rewrite (3.12), which is the general formula for the additive analysis of such value changes, as follows

$$V - 1 = [w(V - P) + (1 - w)(Q - 1)] + \tag{3.20}$$
$$+ [w(P - 1) + (1 - w)(V - Q)]$$

$$= [wP + (1 - w)](Q - 1) + [w + (1 - w)Q](P - 1)$$

In this form the general formula for the additive analysis of the relative changes in the value of commodity aggregates from base year to current year closely resembles the corresponding formula for single commodities. The only difference between the two is in fact that in (3.20) index numbers take the place of the relatives in (3.11). The index numbers of quantity and price in (3.20) are Q_P and P_L for $w = 1$, as in (3.9), Q_L and P_P for $w = 0$, as in (3.10), and the Qs and Ps of (3.18) and (3.19) for $0 < w < 1$. The close resemblance between (3.20) and (3.11) is well worth noting, since it is indicative of the fact that any additive analysis based on (3.20) ensures consistency between the whole and the parts.

3.16 Clearly, apart from the Q_L, P_P and the Q_P, P_L pairs, none but members of the family of index-number pairs defined in (3.18) and (3.19) could conceivably qualify for use in national accounting, because the two conditions from which their formulae were derived are absolutely essential from an analytical point of view in that

particular context. If we also consider it a matter of some importance, as I think we should, that – apart from preserving consistency
between the whole and the parts – the additive analysis should be
such as to be free of bias, then the index-number pair corresponding
to $w = \frac{1}{2}$ should clearly be given pride of place among all conceivable index-number pairs satisfying the basic conditions for multiplicative and additive analysis expressed in (3.2) and (3.16)
respectively. The formulae for this strategically positioned index-
number pair, which we shall denote Q_s, P_s, are

$$Q_s = \frac{Q_L - P_L}{2} + \sqrt{\left(\frac{Q_L - P_L}{2}\right)^2 + V} \qquad (3.21)$$

and

$$P_s = \frac{P_L - Q_L}{2} + \sqrt{\left(\frac{P_L - Q_L}{2}\right)^2 + V} \qquad (3.22)$$

or, more concisely,

$$Q_s = (Q_L - P_L + R)/2 \qquad (3.23)$$

and

$$P_s = (P_L - Q_L + R)/2 \qquad (3.24)$$

where $R = \sqrt{(Q_L - P_L)^2 + 4V}$

It can readily be verified that these formulae for Q_s and P_s are indeed
none other than the ones to which (3.18) and (3.19) reduce if we put
$w = \frac{1}{2}$. Henceforth, we shall refer to Q_s and P_s as the 'new index
numbers', which is the name under which they were introduced
originally back in 1957.[2]

3.17 Since the new index numbers satisfy by definition the condition
for a multiplicative analysis of the value change of a commodity
aggregate from base year to current year into a volume and a price
component, the product of Q_s and P_s will be identically equal to V

$$V \equiv Q_s P_s \qquad (3.25)$$

The new index numbers also satisfy by definition the condition for an additive analysis of the value change of a commodity aggregate from base year to current year to be such as to ensure consistency between the analysis for the whole, i.e. the commodity aggregate, and that for the parts, i.e. the single commodities which form part of that aggregate. But that is not all. The new index numbers are also such as to ensure that the analysis is unbiased. It is these two aspects of the new index numbers which combine to make the difference between P_S and Q_S identically equal to the difference between P_L and Q_L:

$$P_S - Q_S \equiv P_L - Q_L \tag{3.26}$$

as can be readily verified by putting $w = \frac{1}{2}$ in (3.16). Finally, it is worth noting that with the help of (3.25) and (3.26) we can rewrite (3.14) as

$$V - 1 = \tfrac{1}{2}(V - P_s + Q_s - 1) + \tfrac{1}{2}(V - Q_s + P_s - 1) \tag{3.27}$$

$$= \frac{P_s + 1}{2}\left(Q_s - 1\right) + \frac{Q_s + 1}{2}\left(P_s - 1\right)$$

and that in this form the formula for the unbiased additive analysis of the value change of a commodity aggregate resembles (3.13), the comparable formula for single commodities, much more closely than (3.14) did, particularly in its second part.

3.18 In developing the formulae for the new index numbers we imposed two conditions on the additive analysis of value changes into a quantity and a price component; one was that there should be consistency between the analysis for the whole and the analysis for the parts, and the other was that the analysis should be unbiased. If we change either one or both of these conditions we are bound to end up with a different pair of index numbers. One such pair is that of the index numbers of quantity and price which Montgomery (1937) was the first to formulate and which later were rediscovered independently by Vartia (1976), namely,

$$Q_M = V^a, \text{ where } a = \sum w^i_\Delta \frac{\log q^i}{\log v^i} \tag{3.28}$$

and

$$P_M = V^b, \text{ where } b = \sum w_\Delta^i \frac{\log p^i}{\log v^i} \tag{3.29}$$

and where $w_\Delta^i = (V_1^i - V_0^i)/\Sigma(V_1^i - V_0^i)$

The derivation of these formulae involved Montgomery in a very lengthy mathematical argument. However, as it turns out, there is a much shorter route by which these formulae can be obtained. Basically, all that is required in order to find this shorter route is to impose on the index numbers (a) the condition for multiplicative analysis: $V = QP$ (condition 1), (b) the condition that the additive analyses for the whole and the parts should be consistent with each other (condition 2), and (c) the condition that quantity changes and price changes should contribute in the same proportions to the logarithm of the value ratio as they do to the change in absolute value (condition 3). This condition 3, which replaces our condition of unbiasedness in additive analysis, can be symbolised as follows:

for commodity aggregates –   for single commodities –

$\log V = a \log V + b \log V$ $\log v^i = a^i \log v^i + b^i \log v^i$

$\Delta V = a\Delta V + b\Delta V,$ $\Delta V^i = a^i\Delta V^i + b^i\Delta V^i,$

where $V = \Sigma V_1^i/\Sigma V_0^i$ where $v^i = V_1^i/V_0^i$

$\Delta V = \Sigma V_1^i - \Sigma V_0^i$ $\Delta V^i = V_1^i - V_0^i$

and where the first term on the right in each equation is the volume component of the value change and the second is the price component.

By virtue of condition 1, the Montgomery indices must be such that

$$V = Q_M P_M \text{ or } \log V = \log Q_M + \log P_M \tag{3.30}$$

From a comparison of (3.30) with the form in which the multiplicative analysis of value change for a commodity aggregate is shown in the above formulation of condition 3, it follows that

$$\log Q_M = a \log V \text{ or } Q_M = V^a \text{ as in (3.28)}$$

and

$$\log P_M = b \log V \text{ or } P_M = V^b \text{ as in (3.29)}$$

Now in order to determine a and b we proceed as follows. We know that by definition

$$\log v^i = \log q^i p^i = \log q^i + \log p^i$$

From this it follows, by means of comparison with the way in which the multiplicative analysis of value change for a single commodity is shown in the formulation of condition 3, that

$$a^i = \log q^i / \log v^i \text{ and } b^i = \log p^i / \log v^i$$

Therefore

$$a^i \Delta V^i = a^i (V_1^i - V_0^i) = \frac{\log q^i}{\log v^i} (V_1^i - V_0^i)$$

and

$$b^i \Delta V^i = b^i (V_1^i - V_0^i) = \frac{\log p^i}{\log v^i} (V_1^i - V_0^i)$$

Invoking condition 2, by which

$$a\Delta V = \Sigma a^i \Delta V^i \text{ and } b\Delta V = \Sigma b^i \Delta V^i$$

we then arrive at the following expressions for a and b:

$$a = \frac{1}{\Sigma(V_1^i - V_0^i)} \sum \frac{\log q^i}{\log v^i} (V_1^i - V_0^i)$$

$$= \sum w_\Delta^i \frac{\log q^i}{\log v^i} \text{ as in (3.28)}$$

$$b = \frac{1}{\Sigma(V_1^i - V_0^i)} \sum \frac{\log p^i}{\log v^i}(V_1^i - V_0^i)$$

$$= \sum w_\Delta^i \frac{\log p^i}{\log v^i} \text{ as in (3.29)}$$

The fact that Montgomery failed to make use of this short route in the derivation of his formulae makes it doubtful, to say the least, that he was aware of the rather special condition (condition 3) which he implicitly imposed on his index numbers. But even if he was aware of this condition, he certainly did not explain what analytical merit it is supposed to have. His main concern appears to have been to spell out clearly and precisely what we mean when we say that the change in the aggregate value of a group of commodities is partly due to changes in price and partly due to changes in quantity. However, on p. 39 of his book, where he spells out what is meant by these phrases and how the price index and the quantity index should be defined, he admits with engaging candour that his definitions are 'hardly intelligible without the explanations and illustrations we have given'.

3.19   Unlike the hybrid index numbers discussed in Chapter 2 and the new index numbers introduced in this chapter, the Montgomery indices cannot be expressed in terms of V, P_L and Q_L. Consequently, they have to be calculated quite separately from the basic data. Montgomery carried out the laborious calculations involved in order to determine his price index for 1917 (1913 = 100), using the same data as those on which Fisher based his calculations (see section 1.12). The result he came to was 161.74 as compared with a Fisher price index of 161.56. Montgomery rightly observed that this difference is trifling. However, that the difference between the two indices should be so small is not all that surprising, because the gap between the comparable Laspeyres index, at 162.07, and the comparable Paasche index, at 161.05, happened to be a very narrow one. In this particular instance our new price index (P_S), at 161.64, turns out to be even closer to the Fisher price index. However, it should be realized that our new index numbers are not always so close to the Fisher indices. Thus, for instance, we find that the P_S index of UK retail prices for 'transport and vehicles' for 1967 (1958 = 100), based on data in Fowler's study (see section 2.8), works out at 121.15 as compared with a Fisher index of 116.45. (For a general discussion of the difference between P_S and P_F see Note on p. 109.)

4 Properties and Tests

4.1 The new index numbers, which were introduced in Chapter 3, were designed not only to avoid the one-sidedness of the Laspeyres and Paasche measures of volume and price change, but also to meet the requirements of multiplicative as well as additive analysis of value changes of commodity aggregates into a volume and a price component. Having been designed with these objectives in mind, these index numbers have a number of properties which make them particularly suitable measures of volume and price change from an analytical point of view. In this chapter we aim to find out what these properties are, the extent to which they are shared by other index numbers and also whether by any chance the other index numbers have any useful properties which the new index numbers do not have. The method by which we establish whether or not a given type of index number possesses certain properties is the time-honoured one of applying appropriate tests to it.

4.2 The first test which we shall apply is the aggregation test. In the form in which it is presented here this test is due to van Yzeren (1958). For it to be met this test requires that, if for the subaggregates of which a larger aggregate is composed the quantity (price) indices of a given type are known along with the base-year and current-year values of these subaggregates, it should be possible on the basis of this information alone to obtain a quantity (price) index of the same type for the larger aggregate.

4.3 The Laspeyres and the Paasche index numbers of quantity and of price all meet the aggregation test. Where the larger aggregate consists of n commodities ($i = 1, \ldots, n$) and is composed of two subaggregates, the one consisting of the first m commodities ($i = 1, \ldots, m$) and the other consisting of the remaining $n-m$ commodities ($i = m + 1, \ldots, n$), the aggregation takes the following form:

36

for Laspeyres quantity indices and price indices –

$$Q_L = w_0' Q_L' + w_0'' Q_L'' \tag{4.1}$$

and

$$P_L = w_0' P_L' + w_0'' P_L'' \tag{4.2}$$

and for Paasche quantity indices and price indices –

$$\frac{1}{Q_P} = w_1' \frac{1}{Q_P'} + w_1'' \frac{1}{Q_P''} \tag{4.3}$$

and

$$\frac{1}{P_P} = w_1' \frac{1}{P_P'} + w_1'' \frac{1}{P_P''} \tag{4.4}$$

where w_0 and w_1 denote base-year and current-year value weights respectively, and where the unprimed symbols refer to the main aggregate, the single-primed symbols to the first subaggregate and the double-primed symbols to the second subaggregate. In order to prove formulae (4.1)–(4.4) all that needs to be done is to write out in full the familiar definitions of the various indices and weights. Thus, for instance, if we apply this procedure to (4.1) we obtain

$$\frac{\sum_{i=1}^{n} Q_1^i P_0^i}{\sum_{i=1}^{n} Q_0^i P_0^i} = \frac{\sum_{i=1}^{m} Q_0^i P_0^i}{\sum_{i=1}^{n} Q_0^i P_0^i} \times \frac{\sum_{i=1}^{m} Q_1^i P_0^i}{\sum_{i=1}^{m} Q_0^i P_0^i} + \frac{\sum_{i=m+1}^{n} Q_0^i P_0^i}{\sum_{i=1}^{n} Q_0^i P_0^i} \times \frac{\sum_{i=m+1}^{n} Q_1^i P_0^i}{\sum_{i=m+1}^{n} Q_0^i P_0^i}$$

which is clearly true because $\displaystyle\sum_{i=1}^{n} Q_1^i P_0^i = \sum_{i=1}^{m} Q_1^i P_0^i + \sum_{i=m+1}^{n} Q_1^i P_0^i$

4.4 That the new index numbers Q_S and P_S satisfy the aggregation test follows from:

$$V = w_0' V' + w_0'' V'' \tag{4.5}$$

which can be proved to be correct in the same way that (4.1) was
proved to be correct, and from

$$Q_L - P_L = w_0'(Q_L' - P_L') + w_0''(Q_L'' - P_L'') \qquad (4.6)$$

$$= w_0'(Q_S' - P_S') + w_0''(Q_S'' - P_S'')$$

$$= w_0' \left(Q_S' - \frac{V'}{Q_S'} \right) + w_0'' \left(Q_S'' - \frac{V''}{Q_S''} \right)$$

$$= w_0' \left(\frac{V'}{P_S'} - P_S' \right) + w_0'' \left(\frac{V''}{P_S''} - P_S'' \right)$$

since this allows one to write out Q_S in terms of w_0', w_0'', V', V'', Q_S'
and Q_S'', and P_S in terms of w_0', w_0'', V', V'', P_S' and P_S''. Of course, the
aggregation property was built into the new index numbers by insist-
ing that they should be such as to ensure that in the additive analysis
of value changes there should be consistency between the whole and
the parts (see sections 3.7 and 3.17).

4.5 The Fisher indices fail the aggregation test. In order to demonstrate this we develop the formula for Q_F as follows:

$$Q_F = \sqrt{Q_L Q_P} = \sqrt{\frac{w_0' Q_L' + w_0'' Q_L''}{w_1' \dfrac{1}{Q_P'} + w_1'' \dfrac{1}{Q_P''}}} \qquad (4.7)$$

$$= \sqrt{\frac{w_0' Q_L' Q_P' Q_P'' + w_0'' Q_L'' Q_P'' Q_P'}{w_1' Q_P'' + w_1'' Q_P'}}$$

$$= \sqrt{\frac{w_0' Q_P'' Q_F'^2 + w_0'' Q_P' Q_F''^2}{w_1' Q_P'' + w_1'' Q_P'}}$$

This shows us that Q_F cannot be computed on the basis of w_0', w_0'', w_1',
w_1'', Q_F' and Q_F'' alone. Its computation also requires knowledge of
$Q_P'(= V'/P_L')$ and $Q_P''(= V''/P_L'')$. Hence the Fisher quantity index
does not meet the aggregation test. Similarly P_F cannot be computed
without knowledge of $P_P'(= V'/Q_L')$ and $P_P''(= V''/Q_L'')$.

4.6 Edgeworth price indices cannot be aggregated either with the help of no more than base-year and current-year value data, as can be seen from the following development of the formula for P_E:

$$P_E = \frac{P_L + V}{1 + Q_L} = \frac{w_0'P_L' + w_0''P_L'' + w_0'V' + w_0''V''}{w_0' + w_0'' + w_0'Q_L' + w_0''Q_L''} \qquad (4.8)$$

$$= \frac{w_0'(1 + Q_L')P_E' + w_0''(1 + Q_L'')P_E''}{w_0'(1 + Q_L') + w_0''(1 + Q_L'')}$$

The Edgeworth price index for the main aggregate evidently cannot be computed on the basis of w_0', w_0'', P_E' and P_E'' alone. The Laspeyres quantity indices for the subaggregates (Q_L' and Q_L'') are also needed.

4.7 It is worth noting that the Fisher indices do not even meet what might be called the equality test. In order for this test to be met the index of a given type for the larger aggregate should have the same value as the corresponding indices for the subaggregates of which it is composed if the latter are all equal to each other in value (e.g. $Q_L = Q_L'$ if $Q_L' = Q_L''$, etc.). The Laspeyres, the Paasche and the new index numbers all satisfy the equality test, as can readily be verified with the help of formulae (4.1)–(4.6). Indeed, for these index numbers the equality test appears to be nothing but a special case of the aggregation test, which all of them satisfy. That the Fisher indices lack not only the aggregation property (see section 4.5), but also the very natural property implied by the equality test can readily be verified by noting that for $Q_F'' = Q_F'$ (4.7) reduces to

$$Q_F = Q_F' \sqrt{\frac{w_0'Q_P'' + w_0''Q_P'}{w_1'Q_P'' + w_1''Q_P'}} \qquad (4.9)$$

which still leaves the possibility that $Q_F \neq Q_F'$ in case $Q_P' \neq Q_P''$ and $w_1' \neq w_0'$ (and hence $w_1'' \neq w_0''$). The same, of course, applies mutatis mutandis to P_F. That the Edgeworth price index fares better in this respect can be seen from (4.8), which upon putting $P_E'' = P_E'$ reduces to $P_E = P_E'$.

4.8 The results obtained so far rather suggest that any type of index number that meets the aggregation test will also meet the equality test. However, this is not so. Certain index numbers meet the aggregation test, but fail the equality test. The curious Montgomery indices of quantity and price, as defined in (3.28) and (3.29), are a case in point. In order to demonstrate this, one should note first that from (3.28) it follows that

$$a = \frac{\log Q_M}{\log V} = \sum_{i=1}^{n} w_\Delta^i \frac{\log q^i}{\log v^i}.$$

Upon division of the aggregate into two subaggregates, it then equally follows that

$$a' = \frac{\log Q_M'}{\log V'} = \sum_{i=1}^{m} w_\Delta^i \frac{\log q^i}{\log v^i} \bigg/ w_\Delta', \quad \text{where } w_\Delta' = \sum_{i=1}^{m} w_\Delta^i$$

and

$$a'' = \frac{\log Q_M''}{\log V''} = \sum_{i=m+1}^{n} w_\Delta^i \frac{\log q^i}{\log v^i} \bigg/ w_\Delta'', \quad \text{where } w_\Delta'' = \sum_{i=m+1}^{n} w_\Delta^i$$

Hence $a = w_\Delta' a' + w_\Delta'' a''$, or

$$\frac{\log Q_M}{\log V} = w_\Delta' \frac{\log Q_M'}{\log V'} + w_\Delta'' \frac{\log Q_M''}{\log V''} \tag{4.10}$$

Likewise, it can be shown that

$$\frac{\log P_M}{\log V} = w_\Delta' \frac{\log P_M'}{\log V'} + w_\Delta'' \frac{\log P_M''}{\log V''} \tag{4.11}$$

From these two formulae, (4.10) and (4.11), it should be clear that the Montgomery indices meet the aggregation test and also that they fail the equality test – because $Q_M = Q_M'$ for $Q_M'' = Q_M' \neq 1$ and $P_M = P_M'$ for $P_M'' = P_M' \neq 1$ if and only if $\dfrac{1}{\log V} = \dfrac{w_\Delta'}{\log V'} + \dfrac{w_\Delta''}{\log V''}$.
This particular condition is not satisfied in general, but only in very special circumstances, namely,

(a) if both $Q_M'' = Q_M'$ and $P_M'' = P_M'$, for then $V'' = V' = V$, or

(b) if w'_Δ $(= 1 - w''_\Delta)$ accidentally happens to be equal to $\left(\dfrac{\log V''}{\log V} - 1\right) \div \left(\dfrac{\log V''}{\log V'} - 1\right)$.

Consequently, the equality test is not met by the Montgomery indices.

4.9 It will have been noted that all the applications of the aggregation test and the equality test to a variety of different types of index number have been with respect to a split of the main aggregate into only two subaggregates. It should be realised that this was done merely for the sake of simplicity. The results would have been no different no matter into how many subaggregates the main aggregate were split. That this is so can readily be demonstrated by carrying the splitting to its extreme, i.e. by making each subaggregate coincide with one of the various single commodities that form part of the aggregate. For the types of index number that meet the aggregation test the results are the following. The relevant formulae for the Laspeyres indices become

$$Q_L = \Sigma w_0^i q^i \tag{4.12}$$

and

$$P_L = \Sigma w_0^i p^i \tag{4.13}$$

showing that the aggregation process underlying the construction of these indices consists in taking base-weighted arithmetic means of the corresponding relatives. Likewise, the relevant formulae for the Paasche indices become

$$\frac{1}{Q_P} = \sum w_1^i \frac{1}{q^i} \tag{4.14}$$

and

$$\frac{1}{P_P} = \sum w_1^i \frac{1}{p^i} \tag{4.15}$$

showing that for these indices the aggregation process consists in taking current-weighted harmonic means of the corresponding relatives. For the new index numbers the relevant basic formulae become

$$Q_S P_S = \Sigma w_0^i q^i p^i \tag{4.16}$$

and

$$Q_S - P_S = \Sigma w_0^i (q^i - p^i) \tag{4.17}$$

showing that these index numbers can readily be obtained by a simple and symmetric process of aggregation which consists in averaging the products and the differences of the corresponding relatives with the help of base-year value weights. Finally, the relevant basic formulae for the Montgomery indices become

$$\frac{\log Q_M}{\log V} = \sum w_\Delta^i \frac{\log q^i}{\log v^i} \tag{4.18}$$

and

$$\frac{\log P_M}{\log V} = \sum w_\Delta^i \frac{\log p^i}{\log v^i} \tag{4.19}$$

showing that here the underlying aggregation process consists in averaging the ratios of the logarithms of the corresponding quantity (price) relatives and value relatives. All these sums (for the main aggregate) can be written as sums of sums (for the subaggregates). Hence all these index numbers will meet the aggregation test no matter how many of the latter sums are distinguished from one another within the sum for the main aggregate.

4.10 For index numbers used in national accounting it is clearly important that they possess the aggregation property so that, where aggregates are combined into larger aggregates, no inconsistencies arise between the index numbers for the parts (say, food, drink and tobacco, housing, etc.) and those for the whole (say, total private consumption). Hence it is not at all surprising that the Fisher indices for quantity and price – and the Edgeworth price index for that matter – which lack this essential property, have never been used in national accounts work. What is perhaps surprising though is that the aggregation test should have been applied effectively before the national accounts appeared upon the scene. Montgomery, while endeavouring to establish that his index numbers were superior to Fisher's 'ideal' index numbers, in fact observed that his price index, unlike Fisher's, 'may be calculated in a series of stages without affecting the ultimate result'.[1] He proved this statement by showing that his price index can be obtained by applying his formula to the corresponding indices for subaggregates, treating the latter indices as if they were price relatives for single commodities. By doing so he effectively demonstrated that his indices pass the aggregation test, although he did not spell it out in so many words. As for the equality test, it would appear that van Yzeren (1958) was the first to apply this test to index numbers. However, he does not seem to have realised that it was possible for an index number to pass the aggregation test and yet fail the equality test, because he saw what we might call the equality property as 'a natural consequence of the aggregation property'.[2]

4.11 National accounting and the analytical requirements it imposes on index numbers used in that context, including the need for those index numbers to have the aggregation property, were unknown to Fisher and others who occupied themselves with index-number theory in pre-war days. Bearing this in mind, it is by no means surprising that Fisher should have considered the index numbers of the type that were subsequently named after him to be 'ideal' index numbers. He did so mainly because of the properties these index numbers have in common with the quantity and price relatives of single commodities and because of the various tests, both major and minor, which they satisfy. The remainder of this chapter is devoted to a discussion of these tests and their application to the types of index numbers on which attention has been focused in the earlier part of this chapter.

4.12 The principal tests applied by Fisher to a wide variety of possible index-number forms are what he called the 'great reversal tests', namely, the factor-reversal test and the time-reversal test. These tests, unlike the tests dealt with so far, can be applied to quantity and price relatives as well as to quantity and price index numbers. Consequently, they enable us to find out whether or not the various measures of quantity and price developments for commodity aggregates have anything in common with the corresponding measures for single commodities.

4.13 The factor-reversal test requires that the index (relative) resulting from the interchange of Q and P factors should be such that when multiplied with the original index (relative) the product should equal the value ratio. The price and quantity relatives for single commodities clearly meet this test, since upon factor reversal:

$$p^i = \frac{P^i_1}{P^i_0} \text{ becomes } \frac{Q^i_1}{Q^i_0} = q^i, \text{ and vice versa; and } p^i q^i \equiv v^i$$

Unfortunately, the same cannot be said of all index numbers. In particular the most commonly used index numbers of quantity and price – Laspeyres' and Paasche's – appear to fail this test, since upon factor reversal:

$$P_L = \frac{\Sigma Q^i_0 P^i_1}{\Sigma Q^i_0 P^i_0} \text{ becomes } \frac{\Sigma P^i_0 Q^i_1}{\Sigma P^i_0 Q^i_0} = Q_L, \text{ and vice versa; but}$$

$$P_L Q_L \neq V$$

and

$$P_P = \frac{\Sigma Q^i_1 P^i_1}{\Sigma Q^i_1 P^i_0} \text{ becomes } \frac{\Sigma P^i_1 Q^i_1}{\Sigma P^i_1 Q^i_0} = Q_P, \text{ and vice versa; but}$$

$$P_P Q_P \neq V$$

The same is true with respect to the Edgeworth price index, which like its Laspeyres and Paasche counterparts is based on the comparison of the costs of a particular basket of goods and services in the current year and in the base year respectively. Using the formulation of the Edgeworth price index given in (2.6), we find that upon factor reversal:

$$P_E = \frac{P_L + V}{1 + Q_L} \text{ becomes } \frac{Q_L + V}{1 + P_L}; \text{ but } \frac{P_L + V}{1 + Q_L} \cdot \frac{Q_L + V}{1 + P_L} \neq V$$

The Fisher index numbers fare better on this test than either the Laspeyres, the Paasche or the Edgeworth indices, since upon factor reversal:

$P_F = \sqrt{P_L P_P}$ becomes $\sqrt{Q_L Q_P} = Q_F$, and vice versa; and $P_F Q_F \equiv V$

They are not alone in this. The new index numbers and the Montgomery index numbers also meet the factor-reversal test. This can readily be verified, since upon factor reversal

$$P_S = \frac{P_L - Q_L}{2} + \sqrt{\left(\frac{P_L - Q_L}{2}\right)^2 + V}$$

becomes

$$\frac{Q_L - P_L}{2} + \sqrt{\left(\frac{Q_L - P_L}{2}\right)^2 + V} = Q_S$$

and vice versa; and $P_S Q_S \equiv V$;

and

$$P_M = V^{\sum w_\Delta^i \frac{\log p^i}{\log v^i}} \quad \text{becomes} \quad V^{\sum w_\Delta^i \frac{\log q^i}{\log v^i}} = Q_M$$

and vice versa; and $P_M Q_M \equiv V$.

4.14 The time-reversal test, which is the other of Fisher's two 'great reversal tests', requires that the index (relative) obtained by interchanging the role of base year and current year in an index (relative) designed to measure quantity or price movements between two years should be such that when multiplied with the original index (relative) the product should be unity, i.e. the two indices (relatives) should be each other's reciprocal. In other words, the index (relative) should be such that it does not matter in which direction the movement of price or quantity between the two years is measured. In order to save space we shall apply this test only to measures of price movements, but the reader should have no difficulty in obtaining – mutatis mutandis – identical results for measures of quantity movements.

4.15 It is perfectly obvious that the price relatives (and also the quantity relatives) for simple commodities meet the time-reversal test, since upon time reversal:

$$p^i = \frac{P_1^i}{P_0^i} \text{ becomes } \frac{P_0^i}{P_1^i} = \frac{1}{p^i} \text{ ; and } \frac{p^i}{p^i} \equiv 1$$

The most commonly used index numbers of price (and of quantity) – Laspeyres' and Paasche's – however, fail this test as well as the factor-reversal test, since upon time reversal

$$P_L = \frac{\sum Q_0^i P_1^i}{\sum Q_0^i P_0^i} \text{ becomes } \frac{\sum Q_1^i P_0^i}{\sum Q_1^i P_1^i} = \frac{1}{P_P} \text{ ; but } \frac{P_L}{P_P} \neq 1$$

and likewise P_P becomes $\frac{1}{P_L}$; but $\frac{P_P}{P_L} \neq 1$

The Edgeworth price index, on the other hand, fares better on the time-reversal test than on the factor-reversal test, since upon time reversal;

$$P_E = \frac{P_L + V}{1 + Q_L} \text{ becomes } \frac{\dfrac{1}{P_P} + \dfrac{1}{V}}{1 + \dfrac{1}{Q_P}} = \frac{Q_L + 1}{V + P_L} ;$$

$$\text{and } \frac{P_L + V}{1 + Q_L} \cdot \frac{Q_L + 1}{V + P_L} \equiv 1$$

The Fisher index numbers perform equally well on the time-reversal test, since upon time reversal:

$$P_F = \sqrt{P_L P_P} \text{ becomes } \sqrt{\frac{1}{P_P} \cdot \frac{1}{P_L}} = \frac{1}{P_F} \text{ ; and } \frac{P_F}{P_F} \equiv 1$$

The new index numbers and the Montgomery index numbers also meet the time-reversal test, since upon time reversal:

$$P_S = \tfrac{1}{2}[(P_L - Q_L) + \sqrt{(P_L - Q_L)^2 + 4V}] \text{ becomes}$$

$$\frac{1}{2}\left[\left(\frac{1}{P_P} - \frac{1}{Q_P}\right) + \sqrt{\left(\frac{1}{P_P} - \frac{1}{Q_P}\right)^2 + \frac{4}{V}}\right]$$

$$= \frac{1}{2}\left[\left(\frac{Q_L}{V} - \frac{P_L}{V}\right) + \right.$$

$$\left. + \sqrt{\left(\frac{Q_L}{V} - \frac{P_L}{V}\right)^2 + \frac{4}{V}}\right] = \frac{Q_S}{V};$$

and $P_s \dfrac{Q_S}{V} \equiv 1$

and

$$P_M = V^{\displaystyle\sum w^i_\Delta \frac{\log p^i}{\log v^i}} \quad \text{becomes}$$

$$\left(\frac{1}{V}\right)^{\displaystyle\sum w^i_\Delta \frac{\log (1/p^i)}{\log (1/v^i)}} = V^{\displaystyle -\sum w^i_\Delta \frac{\log p^i}{\log v^i}} = P_M^{-1};$$

and $P_M P_M^{-1} \equiv 1$

4.16 Apart from his two reversal tests, Fisher put forward four more index-number tests that are relevant to binary comparisons. These tests, however, he considered to be only of minor importance.[3] They are the proportionality test, the determinateness test, the withdrawal-and-entry test, and the commensurability test. The first three of these are all conditional tests, just like the equality test, which we discussed in sections 4.7 and 4.8. That is to say, they can be applied only in the special circumstances in which the condition on which the test rests is fulfilled. In the case of the equality test, it will be remembered, that condition was that the subaggregates all had quantity or price indices of equal numerical value. Fisher formulated all four of these minor tests with reference to measures of price development, but identical results ensue when these tests are applied to the corresponding measures of quantity development.

4.17 The proportionality test, in Fisher's formulation, requires that: 'An index number of prices should agree with the price relatives if those agree with each other.'[4] All the types of index number considered in this chapter with the exception of the Montgomery indices meet this test, since for $P_1^i = kP_0^i$ for all i, where k is a non-negative constant:

$$P_L = \frac{\Sigma Q_0^i P_1^i}{\Sigma Q_0^i P_0^i} = \frac{\Sigma Q_0^i (kP_0^i)}{\Sigma Q_0^i P_0^i} = \frac{k \Sigma Q_0^i P_0^i}{\Sigma Q_0^i P_0^i} = k$$

and likewise

$$P_P = \frac{\Sigma Q_1^i P_1^i}{\Sigma Q_1^i P_0^i} = \frac{k \Sigma Q_1^i P_0^i}{\Sigma Q_1^i P_0^i} = k$$

Hence

$$P_F = \sqrt{P_L P_P} = \sqrt{k \cdot k} = k$$

$$P_E = \frac{P_L + V}{1 + Q_L} = \frac{P_L + P_P Q_L}{1 + Q_L} = \frac{k + kQ_L}{1 + Q_L} = k$$

and

$$P_S = \frac{P_L - Q_L}{2} + \sqrt{\left(\frac{P_L - Q_L}{2}\right)^2 + V}$$

$$= \frac{k - Q_L}{2} + \sqrt{\left(\frac{k - Q_L}{2}\right)^2 + kQ_L}$$

$$= \frac{k - Q_L}{2} + \sqrt{\frac{k^2 - 2kQ_L + Q_L^2 + 4kQ_L}{4}}$$

$$= \frac{k - Q_L}{2} + \frac{k + Q_L}{2} = k$$

But, from (4.19) we find that for $p^i = k$ for all i:

$$\frac{\log P_M}{\log V} = \sum w_\Delta^i \, \frac{\log p^i}{\log v^i} = \log k \sum \frac{w_\Delta^i}{\log v^i}$$

and hence that, unless $k = 1$, $P_M = k$ if and only if $\frac{1}{\log V} = \sum \frac{w^i}{\log v^i}$ (compare section 4.8 on the application of the equality test to the Montgomery indices). Of course, for the trivial case in which $k = 1$, $\log k = 0$ and therefore $\log P_M = 0$ so that $P_M = 1$ as well.

4.18 The proportionality test is clearly a weaker test than the equality test, since the condition for its being applicable is a more restrictive one. Actually, it is a general rule for conditional tests that the more restrictive the condition for the applicability of such a test, the weaker will be that test. Thus, for instance, for the proportionality test to be applicable the condition is that all relatives must be equal to each other. For the equality test by contrast, it is only the numerical values of the indices for the subaggregates that have to be equal to each other, and that leaves room for the relatives of the commodities within each subaggregate to differ from one another. This explains how it is possible for the Fisher index numbers to meet the proportionality test and yet fail the equality test. A still weaker test than the proportionality test is the identity test. In this test, which Fisher does not mention at all, the k of his proportionality test is given the value of unity. This test is met by all those index numbers that meet the proportionality test.[5] It is also met by the Montgomery index numbers (see section 4.17).

4.19 The determinateness test, as formulated by Fisher, requires that: 'An index number of prices should not be rendered zero, infinity or indeterminate by an individual price becoming zero.'[6] This test is clearly met by the Laspeyres and Paasche index numbers. The reason for this is quite simply that if an individual price becomes zero one quantity-price product term in the summation of all such terms will become zero, but that is not enough to make the sum of all such terms equal to zero. This being so, the test is also met by the Fisher, the Edgeworth and the new index numbers, since all of these can be expressed in terms of the Laspeyres and Paasche index numbers and the value ratio, none of which will become zero, infinity or indeterminate if an individual price becomes zero. Even the Montgomery index numbers would appear to meet this test, since if $p^i = 0$ for given i then for that commodity i:

$$\frac{\log p^i}{\log v^i} = \frac{\log p^i}{\log p^i + \log q^i} = \frac{1}{1 + \dfrac{\log q^i}{\log p^i}} = \frac{1}{1 - 0}$$

$$= 1 \text{ as } \log p^i = \log 0 = -\infty$$

4.20 The withdrawal-and-entry test, as formulated by Fisher, requires that: 'An index number of prices should be unaffected by the withdrawal or entry of a price relative agreeing with the index number.'[7] This test appears to be a weaker one than the equality test because the condition for its applicability is more restrictive, requiring as it does that one of the subaggregates consists of only one single commodity. By the same token, it is a stronger test than the proportionality test (compare section 4.18). What follows from this is that all the index numbers that meet the equality test, such as P_L, P_P, P_E and P_S, will also meet the withdrawal-and-entry test, whereas all that fail the proportionality test, such as P_M, will also fail the withdrawal-and-entry test. This leaves us with those that fail the equality test but meet the proportionality test, such as P_F. For them separate testing is required to determine whether or not they meet the withdrawal-and-entry test. In order to carry out that test with respect to the Fisher price index number, we consider the case in which a n-th commodity with price relative $p^n = P_1^n/P_0^n$ is added to a commodity aggregate consisting of $(n-1)$ commodities with price indexes P_F' and P_P'. Taking the price-counterpart of (4.9), i.e.

$$P_F = P_F' \sqrt{\frac{w_0' P_P'' + w_0'' P_P'}{w_1' P_P'' + w_1'' P_P'}} \tag{4.20}$$

we then find, on replacing the second subaggregate's Paasche price index (P_P'') by the price relative for the n-th commodity (p^n) and replacing the weights w_0'' and w_1'' by w_0^n and w_1^n respectively, that the objection that it leaves the possibility that $P_F \neq P_F'$ in case $P_P' \neq p^n$ and $w_1' \neq w_0'$ still stands (compare section 4.7). Hence P_F does not meet the withdrawal-and-entry test. Fisher knew this, but he went out of his way to play down the importance of the failure of his index numbers to meet this test by arguing that in practical terms it was a matter of no consequence.[8] Of course, what he did not know was that the failure of his index numbers to meet this test was bound up with their failure to meet the more general and more important aggregation and equality tests.

4.21 The last of Fisher's four minor tests is the commensurability test. It requires that: 'An index number of prices should be unaffected by changing any unit of measurement of prices or quantities.'[9] That all index numbers under review here meet this test can be proved as follows. Changes in the units of measurement of prices or quantities do not affect value weights. Neither do they affect relatives, since these are ratios of prices or of quantities and thus independent of the units in which they are measured. Hence the Laspeyres and the Paasche index numbers, which can be written as weighted means of relatives with the weights being shares in the total value of the aggregate in either the base year or the current year, must obey this test. And since the Fisher, the Edgeworth and the new index numbers can all be expressed in terms of the Laspeyres and Paasche indices and the value ratio, which also is unaffected by changes in the units of measurement of prices and quantities, it follows that P_F, P_E and P_S must also meet this test. Likewise P_M meets this test because V, the w^i_Δ, the p^i and the v^i are all independent of the units in which the prices and quantities are measured.

4.22 The nine index-number tests discussed in this chapter are, as far as I am aware, the only ones that are appropriate to binary comparisons and to a two-dimensional analysis of value developments of commodity aggregates. The results we have arrived at in applying these tests are summarised in Table 4.1, where a plus ($+$) signifies that the type of index number concerned meets the test involved and a minus ($-$) that it does not.

TABLE 4.1 Testscores of different types of index number

Type of test	*Type of index number*					
	L	P	E	F	M	S
1. Factor reversal	−	−	−	+	+	+
2. Time reversal	−	−	+	+	+	+
3. Aggregation	+	+	−	−	+	+
4. Equality	+	+	+	−	−	+
5. Withdrawal and entry	+	+	+	−	−	+
6. Proportionality	+	+	+	+	−	+
7. Identity	+	+	+	+	+	+
8. Determinateness	+	+	+	+	+	+
9. Commensurability	+	+	+	+	+	+

What this table shows very clearly is how extraordinarily well the new index numbers perform when subjected to the various index-number tests that are appropriate in the binary context. In fact, as can be seen from the last column of Table 4.1, the new index numbers meet all nine of these tests. None of the other listed index numbers performs anything near as well, nor does any other index number for that matter. Indeed, of the 130 or so different index numbers examined by Fisher none meets more than seven of these tests.

4.23 The combined evidence of Chapters 3 and 4 suggests that the new index numbers (Q_s and P_s) come as close to solving the index-number problem (as defined in section 1.11) as we can ever hope to get. Our reasons for thinking this to be so are:

1. the Q_s,P_s index-number pair is well suited to both the multiplicative and the additive analysis of the value development of a commodity aggregate from one year to another into a volume and a price component; indeed Q_s and P_s were designed with these two forms of analysis in mind (see section 3.16);
2. Unlike the Q_L,P_P and the Q_P,P_L index-number pairs, the Q_s,P_s pair avoids one-sidedness in both forms of analysis (see section 3.16);
3. Q_s and P_s resemble quantity and price relatives more closely in both types of analysis than any other pair of index numbers (see section 3.17);
4. Q_s and P_s, unlike any other type of index numbers, meet all conceivable index-number tests that are relevant in the binary context (see section 4.22).

Part II
Multiple Comparisons

5 Indirect and Chain Indices

5.1 Having dealt with binary comparisons in Part I, we now move on to consider multiple comparisons, i.e. comparisons involving more than two years. The main problem here is how to ensure that all possible binary comparisons between a set of N years are consistent with each other. The value, quantity and price relatives for single commodities all meet this requirement of being consistent with each other, because they all multiply according to the transitive law. Thus for commodity i and any three years r, s and t, we find that

$$\frac{V_s^i}{V_r^i} \times \frac{V_t^i}{V_s^i} = \frac{V_t^i}{V_r^i} \qquad (r, s, t = 1, \ldots, N) \qquad (5.1)$$

$$\frac{Q_s^i}{Q_r^i} \times \frac{Q_t^i}{Q_s^i} = \frac{Q_t^i}{Q_r^i} \qquad (r, s, t = 1, \ldots, N) \qquad (5.2)$$

and

$$\frac{P_s^i}{P_r^i} \times \frac{P_t^i}{P_s^i} = \frac{P_t^i}{P_r^i} \qquad (r, s, t = 1, \ldots, N) \qquad (5.3)$$

5.2 The value ratios for commodity aggregates also multiply according to the transitive law, because

$$\frac{\Sigma V_s^i}{\Sigma V_r^i} \times \frac{\Sigma V_t^i}{\Sigma V_s^i} = \frac{\Sigma V_t^i}{\Sigma V_r^i} \qquad (r, s, t = 1, \ldots, N) \qquad (5.4)$$

But the volume and price indices for such aggregates do not necessarily multiply that way. Thus, for instance, the Laspeyres volume indices and the Paasche price indices, which are used in national

55

accounting as measures of volume and price change of commodity aggregates from one year to another, do not obey the transitive law, because in general

$$\frac{\Sigma P_r^i Q_s^i}{\Sigma P_r^i Q_r^i} \times \frac{\Sigma P_s^i Q_t^i}{\Sigma P_s^i Q_s^i} \neq \frac{\Sigma P_r^i Q_t^i}{\Sigma P_r^i Q_r^i}$$

$(r \neq s \neq t \text{ and } r, s, t = 1, \ldots, N)$ \hfill (5.5)

and

$$\frac{\Sigma Q_s^i P_s^i}{\Sigma Q_s^i P_r^i} \times \frac{\Sigma Q_t^i P_t^i}{\Sigma Q_t^i P_s^i} \neq \frac{\Sigma Q_t^i P_t^i}{\Sigma Q_t^i P_r^i}$$

$(r \neq s \neq t \text{ and } r, s, t = 1, \ldots, N)$ \hfill (5.6)

Likewise the Laspeyres price indices and the Paasche volume indices lack the transitive property and so, for that matter, do all the various hybrid indices discussed in Chapters 2 and 3. Yet, as Westergaard (1890) observed, it should make no difference whether the price rise from 1860 to 1880 is measured directly as between those two years or indirectly as a combination of the price rises from 1860 to 1870 and from 1870 to 1880.[1] Or, expressed in more general terms, a measure of quantity or of price change between two points either in time (say, years) or in space (say, countries) should be such as to produce the same numerical result irrespective of whether the measurement is carried out directly between the two points concerned or indirectly via one or more other points. Any index-number type that meets this requirement may be said to satisfy Westergaard's test.

5.3 Westergaard's test is nowadays better known in an alternative version called the circular test, which requires that a measure of quantity or of price development should be such that it invariably produces a set of numerical values multiplying out to unity if applied to each of a set of direct comparisons which are linked together in an unbroken and closed (i.e. circular) chain. Thus, for instance, quantity relatives meet this test because if we move from r to s and then from s to t and finally back from t to r, we get

$$\frac{Q_s^i}{Q_r^i} \times \frac{Q_t^i}{Q_s^i} \times \frac{Q_r^i}{Q_t^i} = 1 \qquad (r, s, t = 1, \ldots, N)$$ \hfill (5.7)

which is nothing but an alternative way of presenting (5.2).

5.4 All index numbers that are used in time-series analysis meet the circular test, because if they did not they could not be so used. This statement may come as something of a surprise to the reader who has just been told in section 5.2 that the Laspeyres and Paasche indices fail this test, and who is aware of the fact that it is the formulae for these two types of index number which are most widely used in the construction of index numbers of volume and price. However, it should be realised that index numbers which initially are constructed on the basis of either the Laspeyres or the Paasche formula may well be capable of a different interpretation, particularly when forming part of time series. The index numbers which measure the price and volume development of the various commodity aggregates recorded in the national accounts provide a good example of this, as we shall see below.

5.5 In order to keep matters as simple as possible let us consider a case in which only three years are compared with each other and let these three years be the years 0, 1 and 2. Furthermore, let the statistical information made available to us to construct index numbers measuring the volume and the price development of a particular commodity aggregate, such as a country's total private consumption over those years, consist of data on the spending on this aggregate in each of the three years, as well as data on this expenditure revalued at the prices of one of those three years, say, year 0. As we know already, this information enables one to construct Laspeyres quantity indices and Paasche price indices comparing years 1 and 2 with year 0. But what about the comparison between years 1 and 2? Comparing year 2 with year 1 the appropriate Laspeyres quantity index (Q_L^{12}) would be

$$Q_L^{12} = \frac{\Sigma P_1^i Q_2^i}{\Sigma P_1^i Q_1^i} \tag{5.8}$$

and the appropriate Paasche price index (P_P^{12})

$$P_P^{12} = \frac{\Sigma Q_2^i P_2^i}{\Sigma Q_2^i P_1^i} \tag{5.9}$$

However, we are unable to construct these two indices, because we lack the information on year-2 spending revalued at year-1 prices (i.e. $\Sigma Q_2^i P_1^i$). Consequently, the only way in which volumes and prices can be compared between years 1 and 2 is by taking ratios of the appropriate index numbers for the two years concerned to the common base, which in our example is year 0. Thus

$$Q_L^{12,0} = \frac{Q_L^{02}}{Q_L^{01}} \tag{5.10}$$

and

$$P_P^{12,0} = \frac{P_P^{02}}{P_P^{01}} \tag{5.11}$$

where the added superscript (0) denotes the common base of the index numbers from which the indirect index numbers $Q_L^{12,0}$ and $P_P^{12,0}$ have been obtained, while the subscript indicates what type of index numbers these were. The method by which these indirect index numbers are obtained can best be described as the 'base-year comparisons method'.

5.6 Although $Q_L^{12,0}$ and $P_P^{12,0}$ are obtained from Laspeyres and Paasche index numbers respectively, they are not themselves of the Laspeyres or the Paasche type. With respect to $Q_L^{12,0}$ this becomes immediately clear when we expand its formula as follows

$$Q_L^{12,0} = \frac{\Sigma P_0^i Q_2^i / \Sigma P_0^i Q_0^i}{\Sigma P_0^i Q_1^i / \Sigma P_0^i Q_0^i} = \frac{\Sigma P_0^i Q_2^i}{\Sigma P_0^i Q_1^i} \tag{5.12}$$

This shows $Q_L^{12,0}$ to be a volume index which uses year-0 prices to bring year-2 and year-1 values onto a common price base. It is this which distinguishes $Q_L^{12,0}$ from Q_L^{12}, which uses year-1 prices, and Q_P^{12}, which uses year-2 prices for this purpose. As for $P_P^{12,0}$, if we expand its formula in a similar fashion we get

$$P_P^{12,0} = \frac{\Sigma Q_2^i P_2^i / \Sigma Q_2^i P_0^i}{\Sigma Q_1^i P_1^i / \Sigma Q_1^i P_0^i} = \frac{V^{12}}{Q_L^{12,0}} \tag{5.13}$$

This shows that, where $Q_L^{12,0}$ is used as a measure of the volume development of a commodity aggregate from year 1 to year 2, $P_P^{12,0}$

will be the implied price index from year 2 on year 1 for that aggregate.

5.7 All that has been said about $Q_L^{12,0}$ and $P_P^{12,0}$ in sections 5.5 and 5.6 applies equally mutatis mutandis to $Q_L^{st,0}$ and $P_P^{st,0}$, where s and t are any two years out of a series of N years and where year 0 may be any of those N years or any other year for that matter. One of the properties of these types of indirect index numbers is that, in common with quantity and price relatives for single commodities, they multiply according to the transitive law. Thus

$$Q_L^{rs,0} \times Q_L^{st,0} = Q_L^{rt,0} \qquad (r, s, t = 1, \dots, N) \qquad (5.14)$$

because $\quad \dfrac{Q_L^{0s}}{Q_L^{0r}} \times \dfrac{Q_L^{0t}}{Q_L^{0s}} = \dfrac{Q_L^{0t}}{Q_L^{0r}}$

and

$$P_P^{rs,0} \times P_P^{st,0} = P_P^{rt,0} \qquad (r, s, t = 1, \dots, N) \qquad (5.15)$$

because $\quad \dfrac{P_P^{0s}}{P_P^{0r}} \times \dfrac{P_P^{0t}}{P_P^{0s}} = \dfrac{P_P^{0t}}{P_P^{0r}}$

Multiplying according to the transitive law, as they do, these indirect index numbers meet the circular test (see section 5.3) and thereby satisfy an essential requirement for time-series analysis (see section 5.4). Of all the various types of index number we have encountered so far, they are the first to do so.

5.8 For $s = 0$ the indirect volume index $Q_L^{st,0}$ 'reduces' to the direct Laspeyres volume index Q_L^{0t}, i.e.

$$Q_L^{0t,0} = Q_L^{0t} \qquad (t = 1, \dots, N) \qquad (5.16)$$

and likewise the indirect price index $P_P^{st,0}$ 'reduces' to the direct Paasche price index P_P^{0t}, i.e.

$$P_P^{0t,0} = P_P^{0t} \qquad (t = 1, \dots, N) \qquad (5.17)$$

It thus turns out that the volume and price indices which compare each of the other N years with year 0 are capable of two different interpretations. They can either be viewed as Laspeyres or Paasche indices respectively or they can be viewed as 'index numbers' of volume and price for a commodity aggregate of unchanging price structure (compare section 1.7), because that is what our indirect index numbers $Q_L^{st,0}$ and $P_P^{st,0}$ in fact are.

5.9 It follows from (5.13) that

$$V^{12} = Q_L^{12,0} \times P_P^{12,0} \qquad (5.18)$$

which means that it is possible to analyse the value development of a commodity aggregate from year 1 to year 2 into a volume and a price component with the help of the indirect index numbers $Q_L^{12,0}$ and $P_P^{12,0}$. However, this analysis is clearly different from the unobtainable multiplicative analysis

$$V^{12} = Q_L^{12} \times P_P^{12} \qquad (5.19)$$

which is based on proper Laspeyres and Paasche index numbers. It is only when accidentally $Q_L^{12,0} = Q_L^{12}$ and hence $P_P^{12,0} = P_P^{12}$ that the results of the (5.18) and the (5.19) analysis will be the same (see section 5.12).

5.10 With the help of constant-price information based on year-0 prices it is also possible to carry out an additive analysis of a commodity aggregate's value development from year 1 to year 2 into a volume and a price component, because since

$$\Sigma V_2^i - \Sigma V_1^i = (\Sigma V_2^i - \Sigma V_0^i) - (\Sigma V_1^i - \Sigma V_0^i)$$

and since

$$\Sigma V_2^i - \Sigma V_0^i = (\Sigma Q_2^i P_0^i - \Sigma Q_0^i P_0^i) + (\Sigma Q_2^i P_2^i - \Sigma Q_2^i P_0^i)$$

and

$$\Sigma V_1^i - \Sigma V_0^i = (\Sigma Q_1^i P_0^i - \Sigma Q_0^i P_0^i) + (\Sigma Q_1^i P_1^i - \Sigma Q_1^i P_0^i)$$

it follows that

$$\Sigma V_2^i - \Sigma V_1^i = \Sigma (Q_2^i - Q_1^i) P_0^i + \Sigma \{ Q_2^i (P_2^i - P_0^i) - Q_1^i (P_1^i - P_0^i) \} \tag{5.20}$$

From this formula for the indirect additive analysis of the absolute value change from year 1 to year 2 into a volume and a price component, the corresponding formula for such an analysis of the relative change in the aggregate's value from year 1 to year 2 can readily be obtained by dividing both sides by $\Sigma V_0^i = \Sigma Q_0^i P_0^i$. The formula that emerges from this simple operation is

$$V^{02} - V^{01} = (Q_L^{02} - Q_L^{01}) + \{Q_L^{02} (P_P^{02} - 1) - Q_L^{01} (P_P^{01} - 1)\} \tag{5.21}$$

5.11 Formulae (5.20) and (5.21) for the indirect additive analysis of the absolute and the relative change in the aggregate's value from year 1 to year 2 into a volume and a price component clearly differ from the corresponding formulae for the unobtainable direct additive analysis of those value changes, namely:

$$\Sigma V_2^i - \Sigma V_1^i = \Sigma (Q_2^i - Q_1^i) P_1^i + \Sigma Q_2^i (P_2^i - P_1^i) \tag{5.22}$$

and

$$V^{12} - 1 = (Q_L^{12} - 1) + Q_L^{12} (P_P^{12} - 1) \tag{5.23}$$

Of course, it is tempting to replace in (5.23) the index numbers Q_L^{12} and P_P^{12}, which are not available, by the indirect index numbers $Q_L^{12,0}$ and $P_P^{12,0}$, which are available, so as to get a form of additive analysis that can actually be carried out. However, it should be realised that that particular form of additive analysis suffers from a severe drawback. Unlike the additive analysis formulated in (5.21), it is not consistent with the corresponding analyses for the single commodities that form part of the aggregate. Hence it should be rejected (compare section 3.7).

5.12 Wherever the year-1 and year-2 price structures differ from the year-0 price structure, as normally they will, the indirect index numbers $Q_L^{12,0}$ and $P_P^{12,0}$ cannot be guaranteed to be positioned in between Q_L^{12} and Q_P^{12} and P_L^{12} and P_P^{12} respectively. The circumstances in which $Q_L^{12,0}$ and $P_P^{12,0}$ fall within the Laspeyres–Paasche range are in fact rather special. The best way to define those circumstances is to express them in terms of the relevant gap coefficients and their covariance equivalents. (For an explanation of the link between the two see the note on p. 107.) The gap coefficients concerned are the following:

$$g^{12,2} = \frac{Q_L^{12,2}}{Q_L^{12}} - 1 = \frac{Q_P^{12}}{Q_L^{12}} - 1 = \frac{P_P^{12}}{P_L^{12}} - 1$$

$$= \frac{\mathrm{Cov}_{w_1}[q^{12}, p^{12}]}{Q_L^{12} P_L^{12}} \tag{5.24}$$

where $\mathrm{Cov}_{w_1}[q^{12}, p^{12}] = \sum w_1^i \left(\frac{Q_2^i}{Q_1^i} - Q_L^{12} \right) \left(\frac{P_2^i}{P_1^i} - P_L^{12} \right)$

$$g^{12,1} = \frac{Q_L^{12,1}}{Q_L^{12}} - 1 = \frac{Q_L^{12}}{Q_L^{12}} - 1 = \frac{P_P^{12}}{P_P^{12}} - 1 = 0 \tag{5.25}$$

and

$$g^{12,0} = \frac{Q_L^{12,0}}{Q_L^{12}} - 1 = \frac{P_P^{12}}{P_P^{12,0}} - 1 = \frac{\mathrm{Cov}_{w_1}[q^{12}, p^{10}]}{Q_L^{12} P_L^{10}} \tag{5.26}$$

where $\mathrm{Cov}_{w_1}[q^{12}, p^{10}] = \sum w_1^i \left(\frac{Q_2^i}{Q_1^i} - Q_L^{12} \right) \left(\frac{P_0^i}{P_1^i} - P_L^{10} \right)$

By comparing the definitions of these three gap coefficients with one another, we find that

$$Q_L^{12} \gtreqless Q_L^{12,0} \gtreqless Q_P^{12} \text{ and } P_L^{12} \gtreqless P_P^{12,0} \gtreqless P_P^{12} \tag{5.27}$$

if and only if $g^{12,1} \gtreqless g^{12,0} \gtreqless g^{12,2}$

i.e. if and only if $0 \gtreqless \dfrac{\mathrm{Cov}_{w_1}(q^{12}, p^{10})}{Q_L^{12} P_L^{10}} \gtreqless \dfrac{\mathrm{Cov}_{w_1}(q^{12}, p^{12})}{Q_L^{12} P_L^{12}}$

In all other circumstances the indirect index numbers $Q_L^{12,0}$ and $P_P^{12,0}$ will fall outside the Laspeyres–Paasche range, either because the indirect index and the Paasche index lie on opposite sides of the Laspeyres index or because, although being positioned on the same side of the Laspeyres index, the gap between the indirect index and the Laspeyres index is wider than that between the Paasche index and the Laspeyres index.

5.13 Following the same procedure as was applied in sections 1.14 and 1.15 to determine which factors account for the difference between Paasche and Laspeyres index numbers, we find that the relative gap between indirect and direct index numbers, as defined in (5.26), can be broken down into its component parts as follows:

$$g^{12.0} = r_{w_1}(q^{12}, p^{10}) \cdot \frac{s_{w_1}(q^{12})}{Q_L^{12}} \cdot \frac{s_{w_1}(p^{10})}{P_L^{10}}$$

$$(5.28)$$

where
$$r_{w_1}(q^{12}, p^{10}) = \frac{\text{Cov}_{w_1}(q^{12}, p^{10})}{s_{w_1}(q^{12}) \, s_{w_1}(p^{10})}$$

and where
$$s_{w_1}(q^{12}) = \sqrt{\sum w_1^i \left(\frac{Q_2^i}{Q_1^i} - Q_L^{12} \right)^2}$$

$$= Q_L^{12} \sqrt{\sum w_1^i \left(\frac{Q_2^i / Q_1^i}{Q_L^{12}} - 1 \right)^2}$$

$$s_{w_1}(p^{10}) = \sqrt{\sum w_1^i \left(\frac{P_0^i}{P_1^i} - P_L^{10} \right)^2}$$

$$= P_L^{10} \sqrt{\sum w_1^i \left(\frac{P_0^i / P_1^i}{P_L^{10}} - 1 \right)^2}$$

Since it is highly unlikely that there should be any systematic relation between the quantity relatives from year 2 on year 1 and the price relatives from year 0 on year 1, one would expect the correlation between them, as measured by $r_{w_1}(q^{12}, p^{10})$, to be near to zero. Moreover, one would expect the value of this correlation coefficient not to be affected in any systematic way by the degree of proximity of year 0 to year 1. As for the second component of $g^{12,0}$, namely, the relative spread of the quantity relatives from year 2 on year 1, as measured by $s_{w_1} (q_{12}) / Q_L^{12}$, the larger it is the larger the difference between the indirect index numbers and the corresponding direct index numbers will be in relative terms. But the size of this component of the relative gap between the indirect and the direct index numbers will not be affected by the choice of the year that is the base year for the direct index numbers from which the indirect index numbers are derived, i.e. year 0. It is the third component of $g^{12,0}$, namely, the relative spread of the price relatives from year 0 on year 1, as measured by $s_{w_1} (p_{10}) / P_L^{10}$, that is affected by that choice. Of course, in the trivial case where year 0 and year 1 are in fact one and the same year, there will be no difference between the indirect and the direct index numbers (see section 5.8). But neither will there be any difference between them in those cases where years 0 and 1 are different years and where $P_0^i / P_1^i = P_L^{10}$ for all i. In those cases the relative prices of the single commodities comprised in the aggregate will not have changed from year 0 to year 1, because their absolute prices have all changed in the same proportion. In reality such stability in price structure is a rare phenomenon. Normally there will be a change in price structure and the further year 0 is away from year 1 the larger one expects this change to be. And, of course, the larger this change is the larger will be the size of the third component of $g^{12,0}$ and with it (one expects) the deviations between the indirect and the direct index numbers.

5.14 National accounts statisticians normally move forward the year in the prices of which they express their constant-price estimates – our year 0 – every five years or so. Thus, for instance, the official post-war constant-price estimates of United Kingdom output and expenditure have been expressed successively in 1948, 1954, 1958, 1963, 1970, 1975 and 1980 prices. When the valuation base is changed from one year to another, there is usually no attempt made to completely recalculate the various series of constant-price estimates all the way back to the first year in each series. Instead of this, full use is made of the already available constant-price estimates for the earlier years. Thus, for instance, in the United Kingdom series of output and expenditure estimates at 1980 prices, the estimates for years prior to 1978 have been obtained by splicing the already available series of estimates at 1975 prices for these years on to the series of estimates at 1980 prices for later years by the simple device of multiplying the former series by the ratio between 1978 values at 1980 prices and 1978 values at 1975 prices. In much the same way, estimates at 1975 prices for years prior to 1973 were obtained from series of estimates at 1970 prices and estimates at 1970 prices for years prior to 1970 from estimates at 1963 prices. And so on. By proceeding in this way national accounts statisticians not only avoid any revision of index numbers on account of changes in valuation base and all the work that entails. They also ensure that any short-period comparison by way of an indirect index number of volume or price for years that are positioned in between two successive link years will be based on the price structure in a year that is close to the years being compared. That way the danger that the indirect index number concerned will differ greatly from the corresponding (unknown) direct index number is kept to a minimum (see section 5.13). This in itself is enough to make the procedure described in this section preferable to periodic revision of all preceding index numbers whenever the valuation base for the constant-price estimates is changed. But what about indirect index numbers comparing years that are separated by one or more link years?

5.15 Any indirect index number which has been derived from a series of constant-price estimates that has been constructed in the manner described in section 5.14 and which compares years that are separated by one or more link years is in effect a chain index, and that chain index will have as many links as there have been changes in valuation base between the two years the index compares. Thus, for instance, where we measure the volume development of a commodity aggregate in the United Kingdom national accounts from, say, 1965 to 1982 on the basis of the value of that aggregate at 1980 prices in the two years compared, the formula of the index concerned will be:

$$\Sigma Q^i_{82} P^i_{80} \div \left(\Sigma Q^i_{65} P^i_{63} \times \frac{\Sigma Q^i_{70} P^i_{70}}{\Sigma Q^i_{70} P^i_{63}} \times \frac{\Sigma Q^i_{73} P^i_{75}}{\Sigma Q^i_{73} P^i_{70}} \times \frac{\Sigma Q^i_{78} P^i_{80}}{\Sigma Q^i_{78} P^i_{75}} \right)$$

or

$$\frac{\Sigma Q^i_{70} P^i_{63}}{\Sigma Q^i_{65} P^i_{63}} \times \frac{\Sigma Q^i_{73} P^i_{70}}{\Sigma Q^i_{70} P^i_{70}} \times \frac{\Sigma Q^i_{78} P^i_{75}}{\Sigma Q^i_{73} P^i_{75}} \times \frac{\Sigma Q^i_{82} P^i_{80}}{\Sigma Q^i_{78} P^i_{80}}$$

The only slightly unusual features of these national accounts chain indices are: (1) the links are not annual, as they would be in conventional chain indices, and (2) the link years are not always the same as the years that provide the successive valuation bases.

5.16 The formulae for the Laspeyres-based conventional volume chain index of year j on year 0 is:

$$Q_{LC}^{0j} = \frac{\Sigma Q_1^i P_0^i}{\Sigma Q_0^i P_0^i} \times \frac{\Sigma Q_2^i P_1^i}{\Sigma Q_1^i P_1^i} \times \ldots \times \frac{\Sigma Q_j^i P_{j-1}^i}{\Sigma Q_{j-1}^i P_{j-1}^i} \quad (5.29)$$

and the formula for the corresponding Paasche-based conventional price chain index:

$$P_{PC}^{0j} = \frac{\Sigma Q_1^i P_1^i}{\Sigma Q_1^i P_0^i} \times \frac{\Sigma Q_2^i P_2^i}{\Sigma Q_2^i P_1^i} \times \ldots \times \frac{\Sigma Q_j^i P_j^i}{\Sigma Q_j^i P_{j-1}^i} \quad (5.30)$$

These two indices multiply out to the value ratio of year j on year 0, because

$$Q_{LC}^{0j} P_{PC}^{0j} = \frac{\Sigma Q_j^i P_j^i}{\Sigma Q_0^i P_0^i} = V^{0j} \quad (5.31)$$

This result was of course entirely predictable, because the value ratio from year j on year 0 can also be presented as a chain index:

$$V^{0j} = V^{01} \times V^{12} \times \ldots \times V^{j-1,j} \quad (5.32)$$

and each of these separate value ratios, $V^{k-1,k}$ $(k = 1, \ldots, j)$, is identically equal to the product of a Laspeyres volume index and a Paasche price index

$$V^{k-1,k} = Q_L^{k-1,k} P_P^{k-1,k} \quad (k = 1, \ldots, j) \quad (5.33)$$

and the product of all these separate volume indices is equal to Q_{LC}^{0j} as defined in (5.29), and likewise the product of the price indices for the links from 1 up till j is equal to P_{PC}^{0j} as defined in (5.30).

5.17 Given a series of chain indices for N successive years comparing each of these years with year 0, as in (5.29) and (5.30), it proves a simple matter to derive from this information indices measuring the development of either volume or price from any one year (s) to any other year (t) in the series. All that is required in order to do this is to take ratios of the appropriate index numbers in the original series. Thus

$$Q_{LC}^{st} = \frac{Q_{LC}^{0t}}{Q_{LC}^{0s}} \qquad (s, t = 1, \ldots, N) \tag{5.34}$$

and

$$P_{PC}^{st} = \frac{P_{PC}^{0t}}{P_{PC}^{0s}} \qquad (s, t = 1, \ldots, N) \tag{5.35}$$

These indirect indices, which are themselves chain indices like the indices from which they have been derived, multiply according to the transitive law. This follows from their definition. Thus

$$Q_{LC}^{rs} \times Q_{LC}^{st} = Q_{LC}^{rt} \qquad (r, s, t = 1, \ldots, N) \tag{5.36}$$

because

$$\frac{Q_{LC}^{0s}}{Q_{LC}^{0r}} \times \frac{Q_{LC}^{0t}}{Q_{LC}^{0s}} = \frac{Q_{LC}^{0t}}{Q_{LC}^{0r}}$$

and

$$P_{PC}^{rs} \times P_{PC}^{st} = P_{PC}^{rt} \qquad (r, s, t = 1, \ldots, N) \tag{5.37}$$

because

$$\frac{P_{PC}^{0s}}{P_{PC}^{0r}} \times \frac{P_{PC}^{0t}}{P_{PC}^{0s}} = \frac{P_{PC}^{0t}}{P_{PC}^{0r}}$$

Thanks to this transitive property chain indices are well-suited to time-series analysis (see sections 5.3 and 5.4).

5.18 Chain indices can no more be guaranteed to fall within the Laspeyres–Paasche range of the corresponding direct index numbers than the simple indirect index numbers obtained by the base-year comparisons method, $Q_L^{12,0}$ and $P_P^{12,0}$, could (see section 5.12). In order to prove this all we have to do is to consider a chain index with no more than two links. Let this chain index be

$$Q_{LC}^{02} = \frac{\Sigma Q_1^i P_0^i}{\Sigma Q_0^i P_0^i} \times \frac{\Sigma Q_2^i P_1^i}{\Sigma Q_1^i P_1^i} = Q_L^{01} \times Q_L^{12} \tag{5.38}$$

If we compare this with the corresponding Laspeyres index

$$Q_L^{02} = \frac{\Sigma Q_2^i P_0^i}{\Sigma Q_0^i P_0^i} = \frac{\Sigma Q_1^i P_0^i}{\Sigma Q_0^i P_0^i} \times \frac{\Sigma Q_2^i P_0^i}{\Sigma Q_1^i P_0^i} = Q_L^{01} \times Q_L^{12,0} \quad (5.39)$$

we find the ratio between them to be

$$\frac{Q_{LC}^{02}}{Q_L^{02}} = \frac{Q_L^{12}}{Q_L^{12,0}} = 1 + \frac{\text{Cov}_{w_{10}}[q^{12}, p^{01}]}{Q_L^{12,0} P_P^{01}} \quad (5.40)$$

because (as explained in the note on p. 107)

$$\text{Cov}_{w_{10}}(q^{12}, p^{01}) = \sum \frac{Q_1^i P_0^i}{\Sigma Q_1^i P_0^i} \left(\frac{Q_2^i}{Q_1^i} - Q_L^{12,0} \right) \left(\frac{P_1^i}{P_0^i} - P_P^{01} \right)$$

$$= \frac{\Sigma Q_2^i P_1^i}{\Sigma Q_1^i P_0^i} - Q_L^{12,0} P_P^{01} = \left(Q_L^{12} - Q_L^{12,0} \right) P_P^{01}$$

Since furthermore

$$\frac{Q_P^{02}}{Q_L^{02}} = 1 + \frac{\text{Cov}_{w_0}(q^{02}, p^{02})}{Q_L^{02} P_L^{02}} \quad (5.41)$$

where $\text{Cov}_{w_0}(q^{02}, p^{02}) = \sum w_0^i \left(\frac{Q_2^i}{Q_0^i} - Q_L^{02} \right) \left(\frac{P_2^i}{P_0^i} - P_L^{02} \right)$

it follows that

$$Q_L^{02} \gtreqless Q_{LC}^{02} \gtreqless Q_P^{02} \quad (5.42)$$

if and only if $0 \gtreqless \frac{\text{Cov}_{w_{10}}(q^{12}, p^{01})}{Q_L^{12,0} P_P^{01}} \gtreqless \frac{\text{Cov}_{w_0}(q^{02}, p^{02})}{Q_L^{02} P_L^{02}}$

and that in all other circumstances Q_{LC}^{02} will fall outside the Laspeyres –Paasche range.

5.19 Normally one has no means of finding out whether or not index numbers of volume and price which are used in time-series analysis fall within the Laspeyres-Paasche range, because the information required to determine the direct Laspeyres and Paasche indices is not made available. Fortunately, however, it is possible to get some idea about the likelihood of index numbers used in time-series analysis falling outside the Laspeyres–Paasche range thanks to the investigations of Fowler and Fisher. Each of these authors made a comparative study of different types of index number used to measure the price and volume development of commodity aggregates over a series of years. They both published side by side not only direct Laspeyres and Paasche indices to a common base (see sections 1.12 and 1.13), but also chain indices with Laspeyres and Paasche links for the same aggregates and the same years. In the Fowler study, which relates to household expenditure in the United Kingdom during the years from 1958 to 1967, both chain indices for 'All items' and for the 'Transport and Vehicles' group fall inside the Laspeyres–Paasche range for all years except 1962, whereas the chain indices for the 'Food' group are for all years positioned on either side of the Laspeyres–Paasche range. In the Fisher study, which compares different types of index number with each other on the basis of the measures of price and volume development which they provide for the years 1913 to 1918 for an aggregate of thirty-six commodities, the two sets of chain indices fall outside the Laspeyres–Paasche range for all years except 1917. And even for 1917 it is only one of the two chain indices that falls inside the Laspeyres–Paasche range and then only just.

5.20 It is not only the Laspeyres and Paasche indices used in direct binary comparisons that are one-sided measures of volume and price development of commodity aggregates. The same is true of the Laspeyres-based and Paasche-based chain indices used in time-series analysis. Where comparisons are made between adjacent years there is, of course, no difference between Laspeyres (Paasche) indices and Laspeyres (Paasche)-based chain indices, because

$$Q_{LC}^{j-1,j} = \frac{Q_{LC}^{0,j}}{Q_{LC}^{0,j-1}} = \frac{\Sigma Q_j^i P_{j-1}^i}{\Sigma Q_{j-1}^i P_{j-1}^i} = Q_L^{j-1,j} \qquad (j = 1, \ldots, N) \quad (5.43)$$

and likewise

$$P_{PC}^{j-1,j} = \frac{P_{PC}^{0,j}}{P_{PC}^{0,j-1}} = \frac{\Sigma Q_j^i P_j^i}{\Sigma Q_j^i P_{j-1}^i} = P_P^{j-1,j} \qquad (j = 1, \ldots, N) \quad (5.44)$$

Similarly we find that

$$P_{LC}^{j-1,j} = P_L^{j-1,j} \qquad (j = 1, \ldots, N) \qquad (5.45)$$

and

$$Q_{PC}^{j-1,j} = Q_P^{j-1,j} \qquad (j = 1, \ldots, N) \qquad (5.46)$$

In order to find a way of eliminating the one-sidedness from the measures of aggregate price and volume development which appear on the right-hand side of formulae (5.43) – (5.46), we revert to Part I, Chapter 3. There it was explained that the best way of eliminating such one-sidedness in binary comparisons is to use the new index numbers (Q_S and P_S) instead of the corresponding Laspeyres and Paasche index numbers of volume and price. If we do this for each year-to-year comparison for adjacent years, we end up with a new type of chain index which is based on the use of the new index numbers for each link. Thus

$$Q_{SC}^{st} = \frac{Q_{SC}^{0t}}{Q_{SC}^{0s}} \qquad (s, t = 1, \ldots, N) \qquad (5.47)$$

and

$$P_{SC}^{st} = \frac{P_{SC}^{0t}}{P_{SC}^{0s}} \qquad (s, t = 1, \ldots, N) \qquad (5.48)$$

where

$$Q_{SC}^{0j} = Q_S^{01} \times Q_S^{12} \times \ldots \times Q_S^{j-1,j} \qquad (j = 1, \ldots, N) \qquad (5.49)$$

and

$$P_{SC}^{0j} = P_S^{01} \times P_S^{12} \times \ldots \times P_S^{j-1,j} \qquad (j = 1, \ldots, N) \qquad (5.50)$$

5.21 These new chain indices defined in (5.47) – (5.50) appear to be less liable to fall outside the Laspeyres–Paasche range than either the Laspeyres-based or the Paasche-based chain indices. Thus, for instance, all the Q_{SC} and P_{SC} calculated on the basis of the data provided in the Fowler study are found to fall inside the Laspeyres–Paasche range. This compares with less than two-thirds of the corresponding Laspeyres-based and Paasche-based chain indices falling inside that range (see section 5.19). For the data on which the Fisher study is based, the evidence that Q_{SC} and P_{SC} tend to fall inside the Laspeyres–Paasche range is less clear cut. As a matter of fact, none of the different types of chain index calculated on the basis of the Fisher data is entirely satisfactory in this respect. But this is more or less what one would expect, since the Laspeyres–Paasche gap for the Fisher data is extraordinarily narrow for all years in the series, and the changes in the price structure and the volume structure of the aggregate concerned during the war years was very considerable and sudden.

5.22 Another attractive feature of the new chain indices (Q_{SC} and P_{SC}) is that they are normally very close to the direct new index numbers (Q_S and P_S). Table 5.1 in which the two sets of price indices (P_{SC} and P_S), calculated on the basis of data provided in the Fowler study, are compared with each other provides a good example of this.

TABLE 5.1 Comparison of direct and chain index versions of 'new' index numbers of UK retail prices (1958 = 100)

	All items		Food		Transport and vehicles	
	P_S	P_{SC}	P_S	P_{SC}	P_S	P_{SC}
1958	100	100	100	100	100	100
9	100.7	100.7	101.4	101.4	101.2	101.2
1960	101.4	101.4	100.7	100.7	101.9	101.9
1	104.4	104.4	102.0	102.0	102.8	103.2
2	108.6	108.6	105.8	105.8	106.4	106.7
3	110.0	110.0	108.4	108.3	100.1	101.6
4	114.0	114.0	111.2	111.2	105.5	106.1
5	118.6	118.6	115.0	115.0	104.6	107.0
6	123.5	123.4	119.1	119.0	111.0	112.8
7	126.4	126.3	121.9	121.8	112.1	114.6

Even the differences for 'Transport and vehicles', although by no means insignificant, turn out to be relatively small when compared with the corresponding differences between P_{LC} and P_L and between P_{PC} and P_P. Thus, for instance, for 1967 for which $P_{SC} - P_S$ is as much as 2.5, we find that $P_{LC} - P_L = -19.1$ and $P_{PC} - P_P = 6.1$.

5.23 All three types of chain index discussed in this chapter lend themselves to a multiplicative analysis of value developments of commodity aggregates into a volume and a price component, because

$$V^{st} \equiv Q^{st}_{LC} \times P^{st}_{PC} \equiv Q^{st}_{PC} \times P^{st}_{LC} \equiv Q^{st}_{SC} \times P^{st}_{SC}$$

$$(s, t = 1, \ldots , N) \tag{5.51}$$

The propositions underlying this triple identity are the following: (1) for each link in the chain that connects year s with year t the year-on-year value ratio is identically equal to the product of a pair of volume and price indices, namely, $V \equiv Q_L P_P \equiv Q_P P_L \equiv Q_S P_S$; (2) the volume indices and the price indices for the year-on-year links between years s and t multiply out to the corresponding chain indices of volume and price of year t on year s; and (3) the year-on-year value ratios likewise multiply out to the value ratio of year t on year s (compare section 5.16).

5.24 Since volume and price relatives multiply according to the transitive law (see section 5.1) there is no difference between direct and 'chain' relatives of volume and price from year t on year s. Furthermore, as was explained in Chapter 3, the only index numbers which ensure consistency between the additive analysis of the value development of a commodity aggregate from one year (say, year s) to another (say, year t) into a volume and a price component and the corresponding analyses for subaggregates down to the single commodities that form part of the aggregate are the direct Laspeyres and Paasche index numbers of volume and price from year t on year s and weighted averages of the two. Since the chain indices dealt with in this chapter differ from the corresponding direct Laspeyres and Paasche index numbers and since they are not weighted averages of them either, it follows that any additive analysis based on these chain indices must be deficient as far as consistency between the analysis for the whole (i.e. the aggregate) and the analyses for the parts (i.e. the single commodities) is concerned. This being so, the use of these chain indices in additive analysis is not to be recommended.

5.25 That the chain indices themselves are not suitable for use in additive analysis of value changes does not mean that, where chain indices are used to measure the volume and price developments of a commodity aggregate, there is no way of carrying out an additive analysis of that commodity aggregate's value development into a volume and a price component that is consistent with similar analyses for the single commodities that form part of the aggregate. After all, for each link in the chain between years s and t such an analysis is possible. The consistency of that analysis with the corresponding analyses for the single commodities will be fully preserved if the volume (price) components of the value changes of the aggregate for all the links in the chain from years s to year t are added together, and if the same is done with the volume (price) components of the value changes of the single commodities. The resulting additive analysis of the aggregate's value change from year s to year t is an indirect one like that dealt with in section 5.10.

5.26 Every series of index numbers for an N-year period consists of a set of index numbers making $(N-1)$ direct and independent comparisons between either the volume or the price of a commodity aggregate in different years. These direct comparisons may be either comparisons with one particular year in the series or comparisons between adjacent years in the series or any other set of $(N-1)$ independent comparisons. Which particular set of direct comparisons it is decided to use in the construction of a particular index-number series depends very much on what one expects the principal use of that series to be. Thus, for instance, if that use is likely to be the measurement of growth or of inflation since a particular year (e.g. an early post-war year), then of course it would be desirable to construct the series on the basis of direct comparisons with that particular year. If, on the other hand, the series is likely to be used mostly for short-term comparisons, as happens to be the case with the retail price index, then a chain index series might be preferable, since the direct comparisons in such a series are between adjacent years. Naturally, the amount of work involved in compiling the series will also have to be taken into consideration and this may lead to compromises of the type discussed in section 5.14.

6 Other Transitive Indices

6.1 All that has been said in Part I about the choice of formula for the measurement of the volume and the price development of a commodity aggregate from one year to another applies equally where the two situations that are compared with each other are separated from each other not in time but in space. This statement, of course, assumes that, where the latter type of comparison is one between two countries with different currencies, the values and prices in one of those countries will be converted into the currency of the other before the various formulae are applied. The means of conversion to be used for this is the average rate of exchange (r) between the two currencies for the period to which the data on which the comparison is based refer. Where the conversion is not made, the price formula will yield not a proper price index (P), but what is called the purchasing power equivalent (PPE) of the one currency in terms of the other with respect to the particular commodity aggregate to which the price comparison relates. These purchasing power equivalents are widely used in inter-country comparisons. Their relation to the corresponding proper price index is simply

$$PPE = rP \tag{6.1}$$

where $r =$ the exchange rate of the currency of the country compared with the base country against the currency of the latter.

6.2 In accordance with the conclusion reached in section 4.23, the new index numbers (Q_s and P_s) have to be considered to be the best index numbers for use in interspatial as well as intertemporal binary comparisons of the volume and price levels of commodity aggregates. That use, of course, depends on the information required for the calculation of these index numbers actually being available. Where the information is not available Laspeyres and Paasche index numbers may have to be used instead, but it should be realised that the measures they provide are no more than second-best (see sections 3.16 and 4.22).

6.3 Whenever purchasing power equivalents replace proper price index numbers in inter-country comparisons (see section 6.1), the new index number of volume (Q_s) and the corresponding purchasing power equivalent (PPE_s) will have to be calculated on the basis of the following formulae:

$$Q_s = \frac{1}{2}\left[\left(Q_L - \frac{1}{r}PPE_L\right) + \sqrt{\left(Q_L - \frac{1}{r}PPE_L\right)^2 + 4\frac{1}{r}(rV)}\right]$$
(6.2)

and

$$PPE_s = \frac{1}{2}\left[(PPE_L - rQ_L) + \sqrt{(PPE_L - rQ_L)^2 + 4r(rV)}\right]$$
(6.3)

where $PPE_L = rP_L$, $PPE_s, = rP_s$, and
rV = ratio of the values of the commodity aggregate in the two countries compared, each expressed in the units of that country's own currency.

6.4 Having dealt with binary inter-country comparisons, we now move on to consider comparisons involving more than two countries. The basic requirement for such multiple inter-country comparisons is that the index numbers used in these comparisons possess the transitive property (see section 5.2). There are various ways in which we can ensure that this requirement is met. One of these is to apply what might be called the 'base-country comparisons method'. This method consists in first making comparisons between each of the countries concerned and a given base country, and then forming ratios of the index numbers so obtained in order to effect the comparison between any two of the countries under consideration (compare section 5.5). As with intertemporal comparisons of this type, there is a danger that the indirect index numbers of volume and price obtained by applying this method will lie outside the Laspeyres–Paasche range. And this danger will be the greater, the larger the differences are between the price and volume structures of the commodity aggregate concerned in the two countries compared on the one hand and the base country on the other (compare sections 5.12 and 5.13).

6.5　The results obtained by the 'base-country comparisons method' depend not only on the choice made with respect to the type of index number that is to be used in making binary comparisons with the base country. They also depend on the choice of base country. Thus, for instance, if Laspeyres indices are used for making comparisons with the base country (r), the measure for the price comparison between any two countries s and t for a given commodity aggregate will be

$$P_L^{st,r} = \frac{P_L^{rt}}{P_L^{rs}} = \frac{\sum Q_r^i P_t^i}{\sum Q_r^i P_s^i} \qquad (s, t = 1, \ldots, N) \qquad (6.4)$$

However, as any of the N countries involved in the multiple comparison may serve as the base country $(r = 1, \ldots, N)$, there will be N such measures to choose from. Gini (1931) suggested that, in order to obtain a measure that is not dependent on the choice of base country, one should take an average of these N measures. One such average recommended by him is the simple geometric mean (GM) of the N measures:

$$P_L^{st}(GM) = \sqrt[N]{P_L^{st,1} \times P_L^{st,2} \times \ldots \times P_L^{st,N}} \qquad (6.5)$$

$$= \sqrt[N]{\frac{\sum Q_1^i P_t^i}{\sum Q_1^i P_s^i} \times \frac{\sum Q_2^i P_t^i}{\sum Q_2^i P_s^i} \times \ldots \times \frac{\sum Q_N^i P_t^i}{\sum Q_N^i P_s^i}}$$

$$(s, t = 1, \ldots, N)$$

This average index number, which for $N = 2$ reduces to the Fisher price index (P_F^{st}), may also be considered as a transitive variant of that index. As such we shall denote it by the symbol P_{TF}^{st}. Thus

$$P_{TF}^{st} = P_L^{st}(GM) \qquad (6.6)$$

6.6　The averaging procedure of (6.5) can be applied to all transitive price indices obtained by the 'base-country comparisons method', irrespective of the type of price index number that has been used in making the binary comparisons with the base country. For all of them

$$P^{st}(GM) = \sqrt[N]{P^{st,1} \times P^{st,2} \times \ldots \times P^{st,N}} \tag{6.7}$$

$$= \sqrt[N]{\frac{P^{1t}}{P^{1s}} \times \frac{P^{2t}}{P^{2s}} \times \ldots \times \frac{P^{Nt}}{P^{Ns}}}$$

$$(s, t = 1, \ldots, N)$$

Each one of these average index numbers possesses the transitive property, because each one of them can be presented as a ratio of the geometric means of N direct index numbers of country t on all other countries and of country s on all other countries. Thus

$$P^{st}(GM) = P^{sk}(GM) \times P^{kt}(GM) \qquad (k, s, t = 1, \ldots, N) \tag{6.8}$$

6.7 The volume indices that match the various $P^{st}(GM)$ in the multiplicative analysis of inter-country value ratios are also averages of transitive indices obtained by the 'base-country comparisons method'. The matching is the same as in binary comparisons (see sections 1.10, 2.5, 3.17 and 3.18). Thus

$$
\begin{aligned}
V^{st} &\equiv P_L^{st}(GM) \times Q_P^{st}(GM) \\
&\equiv P_P^{st}(GM) \times Q_L^{st}(GM) \\
&\equiv P_F^{st}(GM) \times Q_F^{st}(GM) \\
&\equiv P_S^{st}(GM) \times Q_S^{st}(GM) \\
&\equiv P_M^{st}(GM) \times Q_M^{st}(GM) \qquad (s, t = 1, \ldots, N)
\end{aligned}
\tag{6.9}
$$

where L, P, F, S and M denote the types of index number used in making binary comparisons with the base country, namely, Laspeyres (L), Paasche (P), Fisher (F), new (S) and Montgomery (M) indices respectively.

6.8 Computing-wise average index numbers of the type defined in (6.7) suffer from a serious drawback. They can only be calculated if all the $N(N-1)$ direct index numbers of the same type are known. Fortunately, not all average index numbers suffer from this computing drawback. Gini himself drew attention to a particular weighted arithmetic mean (AM) of the indirect price index numbers defined in (6.4) which, like the average index numbers defined in (6.7), possesses the transitive property and is not dependent on the choice of base country.[1] The weights (w_{rs}) to be applied in order to obtain this particular average index number are the shares of the $\Sigma Q_r^i P_s^i$ in their sum $\left(\Sigma Q_1^i P_s^i + \Sigma Q_2^i P_s^i + \ldots + \Sigma Q_N^i P_s^i \right)$. Applying these weights the index number concerned works out at

$$
\begin{aligned}
P_L^{st}(w_{rs} \, AM) &= w_{1s} \frac{\Sigma Q_1^i P_t^i}{\Sigma Q_1^i P_s^i} + w_{2s} \frac{\Sigma Q_2^i P_t^i}{\Sigma Q_2^i P_s^i} \\
&\quad + \ldots + w_{Ns} \frac{\Sigma Q_N^i P_t^i}{\Sigma Q_N^i P_s^i} \\
&= \frac{\Sigma \left[Q_1^i + Q_2^i + \ldots + Q_N^i \right] P_t^i}{\Sigma \left[Q_1^i + Q_2^i + \ldots + Q_N^i \right] P_s^i}
\end{aligned}
\tag{6.10}
$$

$(s, t = 1, \ldots, N)$

This particular average index number, which for $N = 2$ reduces to the Edgeworth price index (P_E^{st}), may also be considered as a transitive variant of that index. As such we shall denote it by the symbol P_{TE}^{st}. Thus

$$
P_{TE}^{st} = P_L^{st} \left(w_{rs} AM \right)
\tag{6.11}
$$

6.9 The difference between the Edgeworth price index (P_E^{st}) and its transitive variant (P_{TE}^{st}) lies in the composition of the basket of goods and services that is being priced in the two countries compared (s and t). For P_E^{st} that basket has the composition of the country-s and the country-t baskets combined. For P_{TE}^{st}, on the other hand, it has the composition of the combination of the baskets of all the N countries involved in the multiple comparison. In other words, for P_E^{st} the composition of the basket being priced depends on which two countries are being compared, whereas for P_{TE}^{st} it does not vary but is the same no matter which two out of all the N countries are being compared.

6.10 The transitive variant of the Edgeworth price index (P_{TE}^{st}), in common with the Edgeworth price index itself (P_E^{st}), fails the factor-reversal test. Consequently, P_{TE}^{st} and its factor transpose

$$
Q_{TE}^{st} = \frac{\Sigma \left[P_1^i + P_2^i + \ldots + P_N^i \right] Q_t^i}{\Sigma \left[P_1^i + P_2^i + \ldots + P_N^i \right] Q_s^i} \qquad (s, t = 1, \ldots, N)
\tag{6.12}
$$

do not multiply out to the value ratio V^{st}. The volume index number that upon multiplication with P_{TE}^{st} yields V^{st} is in fact

$$V^{st} / P_{TE}^{st} = \frac{\Sigma Q_t^i P_t^i}{\Sigma Q_s^i P_s^i} \Big/ \frac{\Sigma \bar{Q}^i P_t^i}{\Sigma \bar{Q}^i P_s^i} = \frac{\Sigma Q_t^i P_t^i}{\Sigma \bar{Q}^i P_t^i} \Big/ \frac{\Sigma Q_s^i P_s^i}{\Sigma \bar{Q}^i P_s^i}$$

$$(s, t = 1, \ldots, N) \tag{6.13}$$

where $\bar{Q}^i = \left(Q_1^i + Q_2^i + \ldots + Q_N^i \right)/N$

From the final expression for V^{st}/P_{TE}^{st} in (6.13) it is quite clear that this co-factor of P_{TE}^{st} has the transitive property. But then, of course, having been obtained by dividing one transitive measure (viz. P_{TE}^{st}) into another (viz. V^{st}) one would hardly expect it to be anything but transitive.

6.11 Apart from possessing the transitive property, there is very little else that can be said in favour of V^{st}/P_{TE}^{st} as a volume index. It does not only fail the tests that are failed by P_{TE}^{st}, namely the factor-reversal test and the aggregation test. It also fails, for $N > 2$, the identity test and with it, of course, the more demanding proportionality test, withdrawal-and-entry test and equality test as well. This failure to meet the identity test can readily be verified as follows. If $Q_t^i = Q_s^i$ for all i, then

$$V^{st}/P_{TE}^{st} = \frac{\Sigma Q_s^i P_t^i}{\Sigma Q_s^i P_s^i} \Big/ \frac{\Sigma \bar{Q}^i P_t^i}{\Sigma \bar{Q}^i P_s^i}$$

which for $N > 2$ is a ratio between two price indices with different quantity-weights and hence in general will not be equal to unity.

6.12 All that has been said in section 6.10 and 6.11 about P_{TE}^{st} and V^{st}/P_{TE}^{st} equally applies to their factor-transposes Q_{TE}^{st} and V^{st}/Q_{TE}^{st}, because indices that are each other's factor-transpose share the same properties and pass or fail the same tests. Thus Q_{TE}^{st} and its co-factor V^{st}/Q_{TE}^{st} will have the transitive property, but equally the latter will fail the identity test, and with it the proportionality, the withdrawal-and-entry and the equality test, because if $P_t^i = P_s^i$ for all i

$$V^{st}/Q_{TE}^{st} = \frac{\Sigma P_t^i Q_t^i}{\Sigma P_s^i Q_s^i} \Big/ \frac{\Sigma \bar{P}^i Q_t^i}{\Sigma \bar{P}^i Q_s^i} = \frac{\Sigma P_t^i Q_t^i}{\Sigma \bar{P}^i Q_t^i} \Big/ \frac{\Sigma P_s^i Q_s^i}{\Sigma \bar{P}^i Q_s^i}$$

$$(s, t = 1, \ldots, N) \tag{6.14}$$

where $\bar{P}^i = \left[P_1^i + P_2^i + \ldots + P_N^i \right]/N$

becomes

$$V^{st}/Q_{TE}^{st} = \frac{\Sigma P_s^i Q_t^i}{\Sigma P_s^i Q_s^i} \Big/ \frac{\Sigma \bar{P}^i Q_t^i}{\Sigma \bar{P}^i Q_s^i}$$

which for $N > 2$ is a ratio between two volume indices with different price-weights and hence in general will not be equal to unity.

6.13   Although Q_{TE}^{st} and P_{TE}^{st} are each other's factor-transposes, the price-weights applied to the year-t and year-s quantities in the former would appear to be far less suitable weights than the quantity-weights applied to the year-t and year-s prices in the latter, because they fail to reflect over how wide a field each P^i applies. That failure is rectified in a type of index numbers of volume and price which is based on suggestions made by R.C. Geary in 1958, in a note on the subject of multiple inter-country comparisons of the purchasing power of different currencies.[2] These index numbers, which we shall call transitive Geary index numbers, are defined as follows:

$$Q_{TG}^{st} = \frac{\Sigma \Pi^i Q_t^i}{\Sigma \Pi^i Q_s^i} \qquad (s, t = 1, \ldots, N) \tag{6.15}$$

and

$$V^{st}/Q_{TG}^{st} = \frac{\Sigma P_t^i Q_t^i}{\Sigma P_s^i Q_s^i} \Big/ \frac{\Sigma \Pi^i Q_t^i}{\Sigma \Pi^i Q_s^i} \tag{6.16}$$

$$= \frac{\Sigma P_t^i Q_t^i}{\Sigma \Pi^i Q_t^i} \Big/ \frac{\Sigma P_s^i Q_s^i}{\Sigma \Pi^i Q_s^i} \qquad (s, t = 1, \ldots, N)$$

The Π^i in these formulae are 'international prices' which in accordance with Geary's suggestions are defined as

$$\Pi^i = \sum_{r=1}^{N} \frac{Q_r^i}{\displaystyle\sum_{r=1}^{N} Q_r^i} \cdot \frac{P_r^i}{P_G^{ar}} \qquad (i = 1, \ldots, n), \tag{6.17}$$

where $P_G^{ar} = \dfrac{\Sigma P_r^i Q_r^i}{\Sigma \Pi^i Q_r^i}$ $(a = \text{base country}; r = 1, \ldots, N)$

It is worth noting that the prices (the P_r^i) that are averaged in the Π^i are not only quantity-weighted, but also purchasing-power corrected, i.e. corrected by means of division by P_G^{ar} for any price level differences remaining after conversion of the prices in the different countries into a common currency (namely, the base-country currency).

6.14 Since Q_{TE}^{st} and V^{st}/Q_{TE}^{st} on the one hand and Q_{TG}^{st} and V^{st}/Q_{TG}^{st} on the other differ only in their average price weights, the $\bar{P}^i$ and Π^i $(i = 1, \ldots, n)$, it is not surprising that they have a lot in common. Thus we find that all four fail the aggregation test and the factor-reversal test. In addition to this V^{st}/Q_{TE}^{st} and V^{st}/Q_{TG}^{st} for $N > 2$ fail the identity test and with it the more demanding proportionality test, withdrawal-and-entry test and the equality test (compare section 6.12). In this respect the transitive Geary price index $\left[V^{st}/Q_{TG}^{st}\right]$ is clearly inferior to the transitive variant of the Edgeworth price index $\left[P_{TE}^{st}\right]$, which like the Edgeworth price index itself $[P_E]$ meets the identity test and the proportionality test, the withdrawal-and-entry test and the equality test.

6.15 Computing-wise the transitive Geary indices $\left(Q_{TG}^{st} \text{ and } V^{st}/Q_{TG}^{st}\right)$ turn out to be a good deal more demanding than either the transitive variant of the Edgeworth price index and its co-factor $\left(P_{TE}^{st} \text{ and } V^{st}/P_{TE}^{st}\right)$ or their factor-transposes $\left(Q_{TE}^{st} \text{ and } V^{st}/Q_{TE}^{st}\right)$. This is due to the fact that, as (6.17) shows, the $\Pi^i(i = 1, \ldots, n)$ and the $P_G^{ar}(r = 1, \ldots, N)$ are dependent on each other and therefore can only be obtained by solving a system of $(N+n)$ simultaneous equations. (The number of independent equations is actually one less, because by slightly rearranging the Π^i-equations and summing them over all i one arrives at the same equation as one can obtain by slightly rearranging the P_G^{ar}-equations and summing them over all r. However, by setting $P_G^{aa} = 1$ the system can be prevented from becoming indeterminate.)

6.16 In the two-country case (i.e. for $N = 2$) the Geary equations, as set out in (6.17) and further discussed in section 6.15, yield the following simple solution:

$$P_G^{12} = \frac{\sum P_2^i \dfrac{Q_1^i Q_2^i}{Q_1^i + Q_2^i}}{\sum P_1^i \dfrac{Q_1^i Q_2^i}{Q_1^i + Q_2^i}} = \frac{\sum P_2^i \left[\dfrac{1}{\dfrac{1}{Q_1^i} + \dfrac{1}{Q_2^i}}\right]}{\sum P_1^i \left[\dfrac{1}{\dfrac{1}{Q_1^i} + \dfrac{1}{Q_2^i}}\right]} \qquad (6.18)$$

because $\Pi^i = \left[\dfrac{Q_1^i P_1^i}{P_G^{11}} + \dfrac{Q_2^i P_2^i}{P_G^{12}}\right] \Big/ \left[Q_1^i + Q_2^i\right]$

$P_G^{11} = 1$ and $P_G^{12} = \sum P_2^i Q_2^i / \sum \Pi^i Q_2^i$

so that $P_G^{12} \sum \left[Q_1^i P_1^i + \dfrac{Q_2^i P_2^i}{P_G^{12}}\right] \dfrac{Q_2^i}{Q_1^i + Q_2^i} = \sum P_2^i Q_2^i$

and hence $P_G^{12} \sum P_1^i \dfrac{Q_1^i Q_2^i}{Q_1^i + Q_2^i} = \sum P_2^i Q_2^i \left[1 - \dfrac{Q_2^i}{Q_1^i + Q_2^i}\right]$.

Fisher, in 1922, referred to this binary index $[P_G]$ as the 'harmonically crossed weight aggregative' in his listing of different index number types.[3] Apart from that, however, and despite the fact that test-wise it is on a par with the Edgeworth price index $[P_E]$, it went practically unnoticed until in 1958 Geary drew attention to it (or rather to the purchasing power equivalent index corresponding to it). Its neglect until then is presumably due to the fact that, as can be seen from the data in Appendix VII to Fisher's book, it does not necessarily fall within the Laspeyres–Paasche range. In that respect it differs from all the other binary indices we have dealt with in this volume.

6.17 Having dealt in this chapter with transitive index numbers of the Gini type (sections 6.5–6.7), the Edgeworth type (sections 6.8–6.12) and the Geary type (sections 6.13–6.16), there still remains at least one more important class of transitive index numbers that deserves our attention, namely, the van Yzeren indices. Where comparisons are made between N countries they require, like the Gini type index numbers, knowledge of all $N(N-1)$ direct index numbers of a given type (e.g. Laspeyres price index numbers). The characteristic feature of these van Yzeren indices is that country by country the ratios between the direct index numbers and the corresponding van Yzeren index numbers, comparing the one country with all other countries, average out to the same constant. Since, for direct index numbers which are not point-reversible, it obviously makes a difference whether the one country which is being compared with the other countries serves as the base country, or whether it is the other countries that serve as base country in the binary comparisons, it will be necessary to distinguish between two separate sets of transitive van Yzeren indices. If it is the other countries, rather than the one country, that serve as base country, the condition which van Yzeren price indices are made to satisfy is that for all t

$$\frac{1}{N}\left[\frac{P_D^{1t}}{P_{YI}^{1t}} + \frac{P_D^{2t}}{P_{YI}^{2t}} + \ldots + \frac{P_D^{Nt}}{P_{YI}^{Nt}}\right] = c \quad (t = 1, \ldots, N) \quad (6.19)$$

where P_D^{st} = direct price index from country t on country s
$\qquad\qquad (s=1, \ldots, N)$
$\qquad P_{YI}^{st}$ = transitive van Yzeren price index corresponding to P_D^{st}
$\qquad c$ = constant, which is same for all t.

Likewise, the condition which the van Yzeren price indices are made to satisfy if country t serves as the base country in the comparison with all other countries, is that for all t

$$\frac{1}{N}\left[\frac{P_D^{t1}}{P_{YII}^{t1}} + \frac{P_D^{t2}}{P_{YII}^{t2}} + \ldots + \frac{P_D^{tN}}{P_{YII}^{tN}}\right] = c \quad (t = 1, \ldots, N) \quad (6.20)$$

where P_D^{ts} = direct price index from country s $(s=1, \ldots, N)$ on county t
$\qquad P_{YII}^{ts}$ = transitive van Yzeren price index corresponding to P_D^{st}
$\qquad c$ = constant, which is same for all t.

6.18 In his 1956 study van Yzeren showed how to obtain his type of transitive index numbers if the system of direct index numbers from which they are derived consists of Laspeyres index numbers.[4] In doing so he put forward three different methods. The first of these corresponds to our system (6.19), the second corresponds to our system (6.20), and the third is a Fisher-type mixture of the other two aimed at removing the bias inherent in each of the latter. Although van Yzeren restricted himself to dealing with the derivation of transitive index numbers from systems of binary Laspeyres indices, his methods are such that they can be applied just as well to the derivation of transitive index numbers from systems of any other type of binary direct index numbers.

6.19   Our system (6.19) consists of N equations in $N^2 + 1$ unknowns, namely, the P_{YI}^{st} ($s, t = 1, \ldots, N$) and the c. However, thanks to the properties of transitive index numbers this number of unknowns can be greatly reduced. Thus, for a start, we know that $P_{YI}^{st} = P_{YI}^{1t}/P_{YI}^{1s}$. Making use of this relation we are left with $N + 1$ unknowns, namely, the P_{YI}^{1s} ($s=1, \ldots, N$) and the c. But we also know that $P_{YI}^{11} = 1$. Consequently, we are left to solve N unknowns from a system of N equations. It is in the interest of being able to solve this system towards its unknowns in a convenient manner by means of an iterative process that van Yzeren presents this system as (using our notation):

$$1 \quad + P_D^{21}P_{YI}^{12} + P_D^{31}P_{YI}^{13} + \ldots + P_D^{N1}P_{YI}^{1N} = Nc \qquad (6.21)$$

$$\left[P_D^{12} + \qquad P_{YI}^{12} + P_D^{32}P_{YI}^{13} + \ldots + P_D^{N2}P_{YI}^{1N} \right] / Nc = P_{YI}^{12}$$

$$\text{---}$$

$$\left[P_D^{1N} + P_D^{2N}P_{YI}^{12} + P_D^{3N}P_{YI}^{13} + \ldots + \qquad P_{YI}^{1N} \right] / Nc = P_{YI}^{1N}$$

The iterative process for solving this system is quite simple. One starts off by assigning arbitrary values to the P_{YI}^{1s} ($s=2, \ldots, N$), say $P_{YI}^{12} = P_{YI}^{13} = \ldots = P_{YI}^{1N} = 1$. These values are entered on the left-hand side of the equations. Thus we find from the first equation that $1 + P_D^{21} + \ldots P_D^{N1} = Nc$. This Nc-value we also enter on the left-hand side of the other equations. Thus we find the values of P_{YI}^{12} up to P_{YI}^{1N} on the right-hand side of the second to the N-th equation. But these first-round values of the transitive index numbers are only provisional. We use them in a second round, which proceeds in exactly the same way as the first round did with the arbitrary P_{YI}^{1s}-values with which we started. Once the second-round P_{YI}^{1s} ($s=2, \ldots, N$) values are known we use them in a third round and so on until the point is reached where the n-th round results are the same as the $(n-1)$-th round results. By then the system has been solved. Usually only a very few rounds are needed to reach this point. Needless to say, our system (6.20) can be dealt with in exactly the same manner. Also it should be clear that transitive van Yzeren quantity indices can be obtained by the same methods as we discussed above with reference to price indices.

6.20 Van Yzeren demonstrated his methods with the help of the following four-country, two-commodity numerical example.

| Country | Commodity 1 | | Commodity 2 | |
	Quantity	Price	Quantity	Price
A	10	30	2	30
B	6	20	8	10
C	6	25	8	15
D	4	30	10	10

In the remainder of this chapter the use of this example has been extended to a wide-ranging comparison between the various types of transitive index numbers dealt with in this chapter, and between them and the corresponding direct index numbers.

6.21 Table 6.1 shows all the binary Laspeyres, Paasche, Fisher and new index numbers of price and volume that can be computed from the data in van Yzeren's example by treating countries A, B, C and D, each in its turn, as the base country. Comparisons between Paasche and Laspeyres indices country by country, each measured against the same base country, make it clear that the example is not only artificial but also very extreme, because some of the Laspeyres – Paasche gaps turn out to be exceptionally large. For the purpose in hand this is all to the good, as it promises to bring out more sharply any differences between the various indices we are dealing with.

TABLE 6.1   Direct index numbers of price (P) and volume (Q) for countries A, B, C and D based on van Yzeren's numerical example (base country = 100)

| Base country | Price indices | | | | Volume indices | | | |
	A	B	C	D	A	B	C	D
		P_L				Q_L		
A	100.0	61.1	77.8	88.9	100.0	116.7	116.7	116.7
B	210.0	100.0	135.0	130.0	110.0	100.0	100.0	90.0
C	155.6	74.1	100.0	96.3	103.7	100.0	100.0	92.6
D	190.9	81.8	113.6	100.0	145.5	118.2	118.2	100.0
		P_P				Q_P		
A	100.0	47.6	64.3	52.4	100.0	90.9	96.4	68.8
B	163.6	100.0	135.0	122.2	85.7	100.0	100.0	84.6
C	128.6	74.1	100.0	88.0	85.7	100.0	100.0	84.6
D	112.5	76.9	103.8	100.0	85.7	111.1	108.0	100.0

Table 6.1 continued

Base country	Price indices				Volume indices			
	A	B	C	D	A	B	C	D
		P_F				Q_F		
A	100.0	53.9	70.7	68.2	100.0	103.0	106.1	89.6
B	185.4	100.0	135.0	126.1	97.1	100.0	100.0	87.3
C	141.4	74.1	100.0	92.1	94.3	100.0	100.0	88.5
D	146.6	79.3	108.6	100.0	111.7	114.6	113.0	100.0
		P_S				Q_S		
A	100.0	51.8	69.3	65.5	100.0	107.3	108.2	93.3
B	193.2	100.0	135.0	126.8	93.2	100.0	100.0	86.8
C	144.3	74.1	100.0	92.1	92.4	100.0	100.0	88.4
D	152.7	78.9	108.5	100.0	107.2	115.2	113.1	100.0

6.22 Table 6.2 shows series of indirect price index numbers comparing the two-commodity aggregate's price levels in countries B, C and D with its price level in country A, which has been set equal to 100. These indirect index numbers have been derived from the corresponding sets of direct binary index numbers in Table 6.1, in the manner described in section 6.4. All these indices have the transitive property. Therefore, although the indices are presented with a view to comparing price levels in countries B, C and D with the price level in country A, they can equally well be used for comparisons not involving country A. Thus, for instance, if we wish to compare the price level in country C with the one in country B with the help of the first series in the table, we find that for country B's level = 100 country C's level is $100(77.8 \div 61.1)=127.3$. The 'link country' in Table 6.2 corresponds to the 'base country' in Table 6.1. It is the country via which the comparison is made. Thus, for instance, the 64.3 in the second line of Table 6.2, which compares the price level in country C with that in country A, has been obtained from the second line in Table 6.1 as $100(135.0 \div 210.0)$, i.e. as the ratio of the binary indices of countries C and A on country B multiplied by 100. Bearing this in mind, it is not surprising that the lines for link country A in Table 6.2 are replicas of the corresponding lines for base country A in Table 6.1 (in both cases country A = 100). Another point worth noting is that in Table 6.2 the indices shown in the principal diagonal of the 'P_P block' are the same as those shown in the first line of the 'P_L block'. This is bound up with the fact that $P_L^{At,A}$ and $P_P^{At,t}$ are both equal to P_L^{At} ($t = A,B,C,D$) as can readily be verified by writing out their formulae in full.

TABLE 6.2 Indirect and Gini average price index numbers (GM) for countries A, B, C and D (country A = 100)

Link country	Indirect indices for:				Indirect indices for:			
	A	B	C	D	A	B	C	D
	derived from $T.6.1-P_L$ indices				derived from $T.6.1-P_P$ indices			
A	100.0	61.1	77.8	88.9	100.0	47.6	64.3	52.4
B	100.0	47.6	64.3	61.9	100.0	61.1	82.5	74.7
C	100.0	47.6	64.3	61.9	100.0	57.6	77.8	68.4
D	100.0	42.9	59.5	52.4	100.0	68.4	92.3	88.9
GM	100.0	49.4	66.1	65.0	100.0	58.2	78.6	69.8
	derived from $T.6.1-P_F$ indices				derived from $T.6.1-P_S$ indices			
A	100.0	53.9	70.7	68.2	100.0	51.8	69.3	65.5
B	100.0	53.9	72.8	68.0	100.0	51.8	69.9	65.6
C	100.0	52.4	70.7	65.1	100.0	51.3	69.3	63.9
D	100.0	54.1	74.1	68.2	100.0	51.7	71.1	65.5
GM	100.0	53.6	72.1	67.4	100.0	51.6	69.9	65.1

6.23 The sixteen series of indirect price index numbers in Table 6.2 differ from each other because of differences in the types of direct binary indices from which they have been derived (P_L, P_P, P_F and P_S) and differences in the link countries (A, B, C and D), i.e. the countries via which comparisons are made between any two countries in each series. Apart from the sixteen series of indirect price index numbers, Table 6.2 also shows the geometric means (GM) for each four series that have been derived from the same type of binary index. These geometric means are Gini average price index numbers of the type discussed in sections 6.5–6.7. It will be noted that the spread of the indirect index numbers around these average index numbers is much wider for indirect index numbers based on Laspeyres and Paasche binary indices than for indirect index numbers based on either the Fisher or the new binary indices. Also, comparing the four series of Gini indices with each other, we notice that the P_L (GM) and the P_P (GM) series differ widely from each other, whereas the P_F (GM) and the P_S (GM) series, which lie in between the other two, are fairly close to each other.

6.24 Although transitivity is a basic requirement for multiple inter-

TABLE 6.3   Differences between transitive Gini average price indices
and the corresponding direct price indices comparing
countries B, C and D with country A

	A	B	C	D
$P_L(\text{GM}) - P_L$	–	–11.7	–11.6	–23.9
$P_P(\text{GM}) - P_P$	–	10.6	14.3	17.5
$P_F(\text{GM}) - P_F$	–	–0.3	1.4	–0.9
$P_S(\text{GM}) - P_S$	–	–0.1	0.6	–0.4

country comparisons, transitive indices should ideally be such as
to differ as little as possible from the corresponding direct index
numbers that measure differences in price (or volume) levels between
any two countries in the series. Even a cursory inspection of Table
6.2 is enough to establish the fact that by no means all indirect index
numbers are satisfactory from this point of view. As Table 6.3 shows
even the Gini averages of these indirect index numbers are not
necessarily close to the direct index numbers which they replace in
multiple comparisons. P_L (GM) and P_P (GM) are clearly deficient in
this respect. The performance of P_F (GM) and P_S (GM), on the other
hand, proves to be quite impressive on this point with P_S (GM) in this
particular numerical example being the best performer of the lot.
Actually, even the various indirect index numbers that are averaged
in P_F (GM) and in P_S (GM) are mostly very satisfactory in this
respect, with the maximum discrepancy among the former being less
than 5 per cent and the maximum discrepancy among the latter about
half that. This argues strongly in favour of using, where possible,
transitive indices based on either the Fisher or the new index numbers.

6.25   Table 6.4 shows the series of transitive indices which one
obtains by applying van Yzeren's methods to the binary Laspeyres,
Paasche, Fisher and new index numbers of price and volume for
countries A, B, C and D presented in Table 6.1. Comparing these
different series of transitive indices with one another, we find that
as far as the price indices are concerned:

1. the P_L (I) series, i.e. the series obtained by the application of
   method I to the P_L indices in Table 6.1, differs a good deal from
   the P_L (II) series;
2. the indices in the P_L (III) series may be considered to be virtually
   geometric means of the corresponding indices in the P_L (I) and
   P_L (II) series;

TABLE 6.4 Van Yzeren index numbers of price (P) and volume (Q) for countries A, B, C, and D (country $A = 100$)

Based on T.6.1.	Using method	A	B	C	D
P_L	I	100.0	49.4	66.0	65.4
	II	100.0	58.3	78.7	69.6
	III	100.0	53.6	72.1	67.5
P_P	I	100.0	58.1	78.4	70.0
	II	100.0	49.3	66.2	64.6
P_F	I	100.0	53.6	72.1	67.4
	II	100.0	53.6	72.1	67.4
P_S	I	100.0	51.6	69.9	65.1
	II	100.0	51.6	69.9	65.1
Q_L	I	100.0	95.3	95.3	87.7
	II	100.0	112.5	113.6	93.4
Q_P	I	100.0	112.6	113.3	94.6
	II	100.0	95.6	95.6	87.3
Q_F	I	100.0	103.7	104.1	90.7
	II	100.0	103.7	104.1	90.7
Q_S	I	100.0	107.6	107.3	93.8
	II	100.0	107.6	107.3	93.8
Value ratio (V)		100.0	55.6	75.0	61.1

3. the indices in the P_P (I) series are very close to the corresponding indices in the P_L (II) series, and likewise the indices in the P_P (II) series are very close to the corresponding indices in the P_L (I) series;
4. there is no perceptible difference between the P_F (I) and P_F (II) series and between the P_S (I) and the P_S (II) series;
5. the P_F (I) and the P_F (II) series are very nearly identical to the P_L (III) series, but not quite.

As far as the transitive van Yzeren volume indices are concerned, our findings are the same, mutatis mutandis, as the above findings for the transitive van Yzeren price indices. In addition to this it is also worth noting that

$$
\begin{aligned}
V &\equiv P_L \text{ (I)} \times Q_L \text{ (II)} \equiv P_L \text{ (II)} \times Q_L \text{ (I)} \\
&\equiv P_P \text{ (I)} \times Q_P \text{ (II)} \equiv P_P \text{ (II)} \times Q_P \text{ (I)} \\
&\equiv P_F \text{ (I or II)} \times Q_F \text{ (I or II)} \\
&\equiv P_S \text{ (I or II)} \times Q_S \text{ (I or II)}
\end{aligned}
\tag{6.22}
$$

TABLE 6.5 Ratios between van Yzeren indices of price (P) and volume (Q) and the corresponding direct index numbers for countries A, B, C and D (country $A = 100$)[5]

	A	B	C	D	Average ratio
$P_L(\text{I})/P_P$	1.000	1.037	1.027	1.249	1.078
$P_L(\text{II})/P_L$	1.000	0.954	1.012	0.784	0.937
$P_P(\text{I})/P_L$	1.000	0.951	1.008	0.788	0.937
$P_P(\text{II})/P_P$	1.000	1.036	1.030	1.233	1.075
$P_F(\text{I or II})/P_F$	1.000	0.993	1.019	0.987	1.000
$P_S(\text{I or II})/P_S$	1.000	0.997	1.008	0.994	1.000
$Q_L(\text{I})/Q_P$	1.000	1.048	0.988	1.276	1.078
$Q_L(\text{II})/Q_L$	1.000	0.965	0.974	0.801	0.935
$Q_P(\text{I})/Q_L$	1.000	0.965	0.971	0.811	0.937
$Q_P(\text{II})/Q_P$	1.000	1.052	0.992	1.269	1.078
$Q_F(\text{I or II})/Q_F$	1.000	1.006	0.981	1.013	1.000
$Q_S(\text{I or II})/Q_S$	1.000	1.002	0.992	1.006	1.000

6.26 Table 6.5 shows the ratios between the various transitive van Yzeren indices for countries A, B, C and D and the corresponding direct index numbers. In this table the contrast between index-number ratios involving Laspeyres and Paasche measures, on the one hand, and index number ratios involving Fisher and the new index number measures, on the other, is quite striking, particularly for country D, but also for country B. For the former group, the difference between the transitive van Yzeren indices and the corresponding direct index numbers is as much as about 25 per cent for country D, whereas for the latter group the difference is nowhere more than 2 per cent and for P_S (I or II) and P_S, and for Q_S (I or II) and Q_S the difference never even reaches 1 per cent. Of course, it would be possible to construct examples which are less favourable to transitive van Yzeren indices based on the Fisher and on the new index numbers. However, bearing in mind that van Yzeren's example is a rather extreme one (see section 6.21), it would appear safe to assume that transitive van Yzeren indices based on either the Fisher or the new index numbers are normally much to be preferred to any other transitive van Yzeren indices.

6.27 Having made our choice among the transitive van Yzeren indices there remains the question whether or not they are to be preferred to transitive Gini indices. Somewhat surprisingly, it turns out that in practice this question hardly arises and certainly not in the case of van Yzeren's example for which, as comparison of the relevant index numbers in Tables 6.2 and 6.4 shows, P_S (GM) and P_S (I or II) appear to be equal or almost equal to each other. The same appears to be true for P_F (GM) and P_F (I or II). Examination of alternative numerical examples suggests that this (near) equality of P_S (GM) and P_S (I or II) and of P_F (GM) and P_F (I or II) is not confined to van Yzeren's example. Therefore, it would appear safe to suggest that van Yzeren and Gini average indices based on either the Fisher or the new index numbers are probably the best transitive indices obtainable, as they tend to differ least from the corresponding direct index numbers (see sections 6.24 and 6.26).

6.28   There is one matter that has not been given sufficient attention yet and that is whether, in the averaging processes on which the van Yzeren and Gini indices are based, one ought or ought not to assign weights to the various countries between which multiple comparisons are made. Both Gini and van Yzeren discuss the possibility of weighting the different countries in accordance with their respective populations. The effect of such weighting is demonstrated by van Yzeren for the case in which country A is assigned a weight of 7 as against countries B, C and D each having a weight of 1. Essentially what happens in that case is that van Yzeren's methods are applied to ten countries of equal size of which seven are replicas of each other. In Gini average indices population-weighting can be introduced in exactly the same manner. Thus, if these weights are w_r ($r = 1, \ldots, N$), the general formula for the weighted Gini average price indices will be:

$$P^{st}[w_r GM] = \sqrt[\Sigma w_r]{\left[P^{st,\,1}\right]^{W_1} \times \left[P^{st,\,2}\right]^{W_2} \times \ldots \times \left[P^{st,\,N}\right]^{W_N}}$$

$$(s, t = 1, \ldots, N) \quad (6.23)$$

6.29   As can be seen from the top part of Table 6.6, the effect of assigning country A a weight of 7 instead of 1 is considerable for Gini indices based on either Laspeyres or Paasche index numbers, but it is slight for Gini indices based on either the Fisher or the new index numbers. The reason for this is immediately obvious from Table 6.2, where the indirect index numbers that are based on P_L indices and P_P indices are shown to have a much wider spread around their geometric means, i.e. their Gini averages, than do the indirect index

TABLE 6.6 Ratios between weighted and unweighted Gini and van Yzeren indices for countries A, B, C and D^*

	A	B	C	D
Gini indices				
P_L based	1.000	1.146	1.108	1.228
P_P based	1.000	0.894	0.894	0.857
P_F based	1.000	1.004	0.989	1.008
P_S based	1.000	1.001	0.995	1.004
van Yzeren indices				
$P_L(\text{I})$	1.000	1.129	1.096	1.194
$P_L(\text{II})$	1.000	1.121	1.121	1.178
$P_L(\text{III})$	1.000	1.003	0.988	1.007
$P_F(\text{I or II})$	1.000	1.004	0.989	1.008
$P_S(\text{I or II})$	1.000	1.001	0.995	1.004

* For weights see text.

numbers based on P_F indices and P_S indices (see section 6.23). Turning next to the bottom part of Table 6.6 we note that the effect of assigning a weight of 7 instead of 1 to country A is considerable for van Yzeren indices obtained from Laspeyres index numbers by van Yzeren's methods I and II, but that it is slight where van Yzeren's preferred method III is applied. And, as with the Gini indices, the effect of the form of weighting we are dealing with here turns out to be slight for van Yzeren indices based on the Fisher and the new index numbers. Hence we may conclude that, if one of the preferred methods of obtaining transitive indices is used, it does not matter much whether or not the population-type weighting is applied. This appears to be particularly true with respect to P_S-based Gini and van Yzeren indices.

6.30 Having examined in this and the preceding chapter a wide variety of transitive indices, it is hard to avoid the conclusion that transitive indices based on the new index numbers are never inferior and sometimes distinctly superior to comparable transitive indices based on other types of index number. Superiority in this context can mean either one of two things: (1) superiority in the properties possessed by the index, and (2) superiority in closeness to the direct indices which these transitive indices replace when simultaneously comparisons are made between more than two points in either time or space. As regards the first type of superiority, it is worth recalling that all transitive indices that are based on the new index numbers, in

:ommon with those that are based on Fisher index numbers, meet the factor-reversal test (see sections 5.23, 6.7 and 6.25). This makes them perfectly suited to a multiplicative analysis of value ratios of commodity aggregates between different years or different countries into a volume and a price component. Where transitive indices are obtained by applying either the base-year comparisons method or the chain index method, it even proves possible, if these transitive indices are based on the new index numbers, to provide an indirect additive analysis of aggregate value changes over time which is consistent with the corresponding analyses for the single commodities that form part of the aggregate (see sections 5.10 and 5.25). As for the second type of superiority, we have found that transitive indices which are based on the new index numbers are almost invariably exceedingly close to the direct indices which they replace when comparisons are made simultaneously between more than two points in time or space (see sections 5.22, 6.23, 6.24 and 6.26). Indeed, the fact that transitive indices based on the new index numbers and obtained in such different ways as Gini's method (section 6.6) and van Yzeren's methods I and II (section 6.17) produce results which do not differ perceptibly leads one to suspect that it may prove impossible to construct any other transitive indices (with the possible exception of those based on Fisher index numbers) which are even closer to the direct index numbers they replace (see section 6.27). Interestingly, it turns out that these indices are also only very little affected by country-weighting (see section 6.29).

6.31 Which of the various type of transitive index based on the new index numbers should be used in any particular case depends on a couple of conflicting considerations. The simplest forms of transitive indices are series of indirect index numbers obtained by base-year or base-country comparisons methods (sections 5.5 and 6.4). But, in the nature of things, these indirect index numbers are dependent on the choice made with respect to the year or country that is the base year or base country of the series of direct index numbers from which the series of indirect index numbers is derived. The Gini and van Yzeren methods are aimed at eliminating this dependence on the choice of base year or base country. But the cost of achieving this object is a high one, namely, knowledge of all $N(N-1)$ direct index numbers concerned linking each of the N years or countries involved with each of the others. In making multiple inter-country comparisons it is often considered worth paying this price. This is quite understandable, particularly where the results of such comparisons are to form the basis for establishing comparable salary levels for members of the staff of multinational companies and international organisations located in different countries, and for burden-sharing exercises of international economic and defence organisations. In making multiple intertemporal comparisons the price to be paid for making the results of the comparisons independent of the choice of base year will almost invariably be considered too high. The reason for this is that, for years that are not too far apart, price and volume structures will normally not differ sufficiently for it to make any noticeable difference on the structures for which of the years involved in the exercise the new index numbers are based (see section 5.22). A change of base year every five, or even ten, years will normally be quite sufficient to ensure that the transitive indices based on series of new index numbers do not depart too far from the Gini or van Yzeren 'neutral' indices.

6.32   Where the number of countries involved in a multiple intercountry comparison is large, the price to be paid for obtaining Gini or van Yzeren transitive indices may well be judged excessive. The question then arises whether in those circumstances one should use just one of the N possible series of indirect index numbers based on the new index numbers, or whether one should use instead transitive index numbers of either the Edgeworth or the Geary type (see sections 6.8 and 6.13). Table 6.7, which is based on the van Yzeren example (section 6.20), suggests that once again the advantage appears to lie on the side of transitive index numbers based on the new index numbers.

Comparison of the ratio-series in the bottom part of the table shows that of the transitive indices that are not dependent on the choice of base country

1. $P_{TE}^{st} = P_L^{st} \left[w_{rs} AM \right]$ (see section 6.8) gives practically the same results as P_L^{st} (GM) and
2. P_{TG}^{st} gives results that are even further removed from P_S^{st} (GM) than P_P^{st} (GM), which proved to be further removed from P_S^{st} (GM) than any of the other Gini indices.

Thus, after having examined a fairly wide variety of transitive indices we come to the conclusion, maybe somewhat surprisingly, that the

TABLE 6.7 Ratios between various transitive price indices and P_S(GM) for countries A, B, C and D (country $A = 100$)

	A	B	C	D
Indirect indices P_S based Link country				
A	1.000	1.002	0.992	1.006
B	1.000	1.002	1.000	1.008
C	1.000	0.994	0.992	0.981
D	1.000	1.001	1.017	1.006
P_{TE}	1.000	0.956	0.945	1.005
$P_{TG}(= V/Q_{TG})$	1.000	1.167	1.164	1.124
P_L(GM)	1.000	0.956	0.946	0.998
P_P(GM)	1.000	1.127	1.124	1.073

new index numbers are not only best in the binary context, but also that the various types of transitive indices based on them are on the whole to be preferred to all others.

Part III
Miscellaneous Notes

Irving Fisher's Search for the Ideal Index Number

After a thorough investigation in his book on *The Making of Index Numbers*, Irving Fisher arrived at the conclusion that the geometric mean of the Laspeyres and Paasche index numbers was the 'ideal' index number. It is a matter of some interest to follow the route by which Fisher reached this conclusion and to find out whether it was in every respect the best possible route.

In an attempt to cover as many different types of index number as possible in his study Fisher started off with developing forty-six primary formulae. These were obtained by combining the price (or volume) relatives of the single commodities into index numbers with the help of five different types of average, namely, the arithmetic, harmonic and geometric means and the median and the mode, and five different sets of weights, namely, equal weights and the shares in $\Sigma P_0^i Q_0^i$, $\Sigma P_0^i Q_1^i$, $\Sigma P_1^i Q_0^i$ and $\Sigma P_1^i Q_1^i$ respectively, and by adding to the formulae for these index numbers the formulae for their factor antitheses (which can be obtained in the way that has been described in section 2.7). Also included among the forty-six primary formulae were the ratio of the unweighted current-year and base-year sums of prices (or quantities) and its factor antithesis. To these 46 primary formulae Fisher added, apart from a few broadened-base and constant-weight formulae, a further eighty-four index-number formulae which were obtained by the traditional approach of averaging formulae or weights. Actually, no less than fifty of these additional eighty-four formulae were obtained by the 'crossing' of primary formulae, where 'crossing' means taking the geometric mean of two formulae, and a further four were obtained by the crossing of such crosses. Also included were P (AM) and its factor antithesis (as we defined them in sections 2.1 and 2.7). The remaining twenty-eight additional formulae were 'cross-weighted' formulae (like P_E), their factor antitheses and crosses between them. The term 'cross-weighted' is used here in the sense in which Fisher used it. That is to say it covers not only the geometric but also the arithmetic and the harmonic crossing of the weights of two formulae. Moreover, the use of the term 'weights' is not confined to the weights attached to price (or quantity) relatives in index-number construction. Fisher uses the term as well for the quantities of single commodities in those cases where the index number is of the aggregative type, i.e. where it is based on a comparison between the value of a given commodity basket in the current year and in the base year respectively. Thus, in Fisher's terminology, P_F is a 'cross' between P_L and P_P, whereas P_E is the 'arithmetically crossed weight aggregative' of P_L and P_P.

In his search for the ideal index-number formula, Fisher first eliminated from his list of 130 different types of index number (excluding the broadened-base and constant-weight types) all the simple (i.e. unweighted or equal-weighted) index numbers and their derivatives (i.e. factor antitheses and crosses), because their weighting is freakish and this causes them to produce highly erratic results. Likewise, he eliminated all modal and median-type index numbers and their derivatives (including some cross-weighted ones), because mode and median are freakish types of average which tend to be unresponsive to small changes in the data. This elimination of freakish index-number formulae reduced the list of formulae by half.

Fisher's next step was to eliminate from the remaining sixty-five formulae another twenty because they produce index numbers which are biased in one direction or the other. Such bias has its origin in either the type of average used or the type of weight used, or both; arithmetic means produce an upward and harmonic means produce a downward bias, and likewise the $Q_1^i P_1^i$ and $Q_0^i P_1^i$ ($Q_1^i P_1^i$ and $Q_1^i P_0^i$) weighting systems impart an upward and the $Q_0^i P_0^i$ and $Q_1^i P_0^i$ ($Q_0^i P_0^i$ and $Q_0^i P_1^i$) weighting systems impart a downward bias to price (volume) index numbers.

Neither the Laspeyres nor the Paasche index numbers were eliminated from Fisher's list on the grounds of bias, because for P_L and P_P (and for Q_L and Q_P) the type-bias and the weight-bias are in opposite directions. Actually P_L and P_P were the only two primary price index numbers left in Fisher's list of index numbers that were neither freakish nor biased.

What Fisher regarded as the most remarkable feature of the forty-five types of index number that remained on his list after the freakish and the biased types had been eliminated, was the fact that they practically all agreed with each other when calculated for a group of commodities that displayed widely differing price (and volume) developments. But he went on to observe that there existed an even closer agreement between the results obtained by the use of the thirteen index numbers, among these forty-five, which meet both his factor-reversal test and his time-reversal test.

When it came to choosing the 'ideal' index-number formula from among the thirteen formulae that still remained on his list after he had applied his two reversal tests, Fisher became, on his own admission, 'much less definite and sure' in his argument. This is demonstrated by the fact that for his final choice he relied heavily on such propositions as 'weight crossing of any kind is probably not as accurate a splitter of differences as formula crossing' and 'two equally promising estimates or measures may probably be improved in accuracy by taking their average'. Finally, having selected P_F (and Q_F) as the ideal index-number form on grounds such as these, he also praised this index-number type for its algebraic simplicity and the ease and speed with which it can be computed.

It is somewhat surprising that Fisher did not make better use of the test approach to the selection of index-number formulae, because if he had brought not only his two reversal tests but also his proportionality test into play, he could instantly have narrowed down the search for the 'ideal' formula to the following four: (1) $\left[P_L\frac{V}{Q_L}\right]^{\frac{1}{2}}$, (2) $\left[P_W\frac{V}{Q_W}\right]^{\frac{1}{2}}$, (3) $\left[P_E\frac{V}{Q_E}\right]^{\frac{1}{2}}$ and (4) $\left[P_G\frac{V}{Q_G}\right]^{\frac{1}{2}}$, where P_W, P_E and P_G are the geometrically, the arithmetically and the harmonically crossed weight aggregative price indices respectively. Test-wise there is nothing to choose between these four formulae (which in Fisher's list carry the numbers 353, 1353, 2353 and 3353), because all four meet the determinateness test and all four equally fail the withdrawal-and-entry test, but on account of its algebraic simplicity the first P_F is clearly much to be preferred to the other three.

On reading Fisher's book one gets the impression that he was a little too anxious to demonstrate that index numbers are respectable measures of aggregate price and volume developments. In order to achieve this object he made great play of the fact that the numerical results obtained by the use of the forty-five index-number formulae remaining after freakish and biased index number types had been excluded 'agree more closely than the standards of ordinary statistical practice require'.[1] As the Laspeyres and Paasche formulae were among these forty-five he did little to encourage practising statisticians to base their calculations on the formulae for the index numbers he preferred and to which his name became attached (P_F and Q_F).

Banerjee's Factorial Index Numbers

The underlying idea of Banerjee's so-called factorial approach to the construction of index numbers[1] appears to be that if commodity aggregates, like single commodities, had a price measure and a volume measure of their own, then these measures (which we shall denote by symbols with an asterisk) should be such that

$$P_j^* Q_k^* = \Sigma P_j^i Q_k^i \qquad (j, k = 0, 1)$$

and the index numbers of price and volume based on them should be

$$P = P_1^*/P_0^* \text{ and } Q = Q_1^*/Q_0^*$$

Forming (as in factorial design analysis) the products

$$\left[P_1^* + P_0^*\right]\left[Q_1^* + Q_0^*\right] = a$$

$$\left[P_1^* - P_0^*\right]\left[Q_1^* + Q_0^*\right] = b$$

$$\left[P_1^* + P_0^*\right]\left[Q_1^* - Q_0^*\right] = c$$

$$\left[P_1^* - P_0^*\right]\left[Q_1^* - Q_0^*\right] = d$$

and dividing them by $V_o = P_0^* Q_0^* = \Sigma P_o^i Q_o^i$ Banerjee then concludes that the aggregate price and volume indices should be such that

$$(P + 1)(Q + 1) \equiv V + P_L + Q_L + 1 \equiv a/V_0$$

$$(P - 1)(Q + 1) \equiv V + P_L - Q_L - 1 \equiv b/V_0$$

$$(P + 1)(Q - 1) \equiv V - P_L + Q_L - 1 \equiv c/V_0$$

$$(P - 1)(Q - 1) \equiv V - P_L - Q_L + 1 \equiv d/V_0$$

It is at this point that it becomes clear that the underlying idea of the factorial approach is erroneous, because there exist no P, Q pair that can satisfy simultaneously all four of these relations. Taking the relations two by two and solving them towards P and Q we actually end up with no less than six different P, Q pairs. Thus, for instance, combining the first and the second relation we find $P(a, b) = P_E$ and $Q(a, b) = Q_L$, whereas if we combine the first and the third relation we find $P(a, c) = P_L$ and $Q(a, c) = Q_E$. Of the six different P, Q pairs one, namely $P(a, d)$ $Q(a, d)$, is unusable because (1) upon factor reversal the first and fourth relation stay the same and therefore it is impossible to decide, upon solving towards P and Q, which of the two roots

$$\frac{P_L + Q_L}{2} \pm \sqrt{\left[\frac{P_L + Q_L}{2}\right]^2 - V}$$

is P and which is Q, and (2) the expression under the square root sign can be negative in which case neither P nor Q is a real number. Of the five remaining P, Q pairs, all but one fail to multiply out to the money-value ratio (V) as they should have done if the underlying idea of the factorial approach had been correct. Hence they must be considered unacceptable from an analytical point of view. Thus we are left with only one usable and acceptable P, Q pair and that particular pair, $P(b, c)$, $Q(b, c)$, turns out to be the pair of the new index numbers, P_S, Q_S, which we discussed in Chapter 3 and the remarkable properties of which were highlighted in Chapter 4.

It is also somewhat doubtful whether Banerjee's claim that 'the factorial approach . . . provides a new interpretation to some of the known indexes,'[2] is fully justified. Personally, I think it is not, because I fail to see that there is a clear correspondence between a 2^2-factorial experiment (i.e. an experiment involving two factors at two levels each, say, in agriculture) and the analysis of the value development of a commodity aggregate from, say, one year to another into a price and a volume component. In particular, I find it hard to conceive of the n associated price and volume changes of the n single commodities in the aggregate ($i = 1, \ldots, n$) as replications of each other, in the sense of which the term 'replication' is understood in randomised block design experiments. In the latter, the experiments carried out on the various blocks (each of which consists of a given number of plots of land) are identical to each other, and the object of averaging the results of these replicated experiments is to eliminate (hopefully) the effect of other factors that are not deliberately varied in these experiments.[3]

The Comparative Proportionality Test

Of all the many types of index number examined by Irving Fisher none satisfies all the tests he designed (see p. 101); even the one he selected as being the best fails one of his tests. In view of this, it is surprising to find that the new index numbers, P_S and Q_S, satisfy all Fisher's tests and the important aggregation test as well (see Table 4.1) Given the non-uniqueness of index-number measures of volume and price developments of commodity aggregates from base year to current year, this extraordinary performance of the new index numbers leads one to suspect that there must be one or more other tests on which P_S and Q_S fare worse. Some attempts have been made at formulating at least one such test. As a result of this we now have a test which requires that, if all current-year prices are multiplied by a constant factor k and all base-year prices as well as base-year and current-year quantities are left unchanged, then the price index should be multiplied by k and the quantity index should remain unchanged. In order to avoid confusion with Fisher's proportionality test, we shall call this test the comparative proportionality test.

By replacing P_1^i by kP_1^i for every i and by denoting the resulting index numbers by primed symbols, we find that

$$P_L' = \frac{\Sigma Q_0^i(kP_1^i)}{\Sigma Q_0^i P_0^i} = k\frac{\Sigma Q_0^i P_1^i}{\Sigma Q_0^i P_0^i} = kP_L \text{ and } Q_L' = \frac{\Sigma Q_1^i P_0^i}{\Sigma Q_0^i P_0^i} = Q_L$$

$$P_P' = \frac{\Sigma Q_1^i(kP_1^i)}{\Sigma Q_1^i P_0^i} = k\frac{\Sigma Q_1^i P_1^i}{\Sigma Q_1^i P_0^i} = kP_P \text{ and}$$

$$Q_P' = \frac{\Sigma Q_1^i(kP_1^i)}{\Sigma Q_0^i(kP_1^i)} = \frac{\Sigma Q_1^i P_1^i}{\Sigma Q_0^i P_1^i} = Q_P$$

$$P_F' = \sqrt{P_L' P_P'} = \sqrt{[kP_L][kP_P]} = k\sqrt{P_L P_P} = kP_F \text{ and}$$

$$Q_F' = \sqrt{Q_L' Q_P'} = \sqrt{Q_L Q_P} = Q_F$$

$$P'_E = \frac{P'_L + V'}{1 + Q'_L} = \frac{k(P_L + V)}{1 + Q_L} = kP_E \text{ as}$$

$$V' = \frac{\Sigma Q_1^i(kP_1^i)}{\Sigma Q_0^i P_0^i} = k\frac{\Sigma Q_1^i P_1^i}{\Sigma Q_0^i P_0^i} = kV$$

but

$$P'_S = \frac{P'_L - Q'_L}{2} + \sqrt{\left[\frac{P'_L - Q'_L}{2}\right]^2 + V'} = \frac{kP_L - Q_L}{2} + \sqrt{\left[\frac{kP_L - Q_L}{2}\right]^2 + kV}$$

$$\neq \frac{kP_L - kQ_L}{2} + \sqrt{\left[\frac{kP_L - kQ_L}{2}\right]^2 + k^2V} = kP_S$$

since $Q'_L = Q_L \neq kQ_L$ and $V' = kV \neq k^2V$, except if, trivially, $k = 1$; and likewise

$$Q'_S = \frac{Q'_L - P'_L}{2} + \sqrt{\left[\frac{Q'_L - P'_L}{2}\right]^2 + V'}$$

$$= \frac{Q_L - kP_L}{2} + \sqrt{\left[\frac{Q_L - kP_L}{2}\right]^2 + kV} \neq Q_S$$

The fact that the Montgomery index numbers also fail this test is a point that need not deter us any further here, since we are principally concerned with the new index numbers at present.

The failure of the new index numbers to satisfy the comparative proportionality test is not as serious as one might imagine. The reason for this is the following. Unlike Fisher's proportionality test, which deals with the case in which all prices change by a constant factor k from base year to current year, the comparative proportionality test deals with the case in which two different current-year situations are compared with the base-year situation. The difference between these two current-year situations is that in the one the prices of the single commodities in the aggregate are k times what they are in the other. Such a difference can only arise in one of two ways and neither of these is really relevant in the binary context.

The first way to create the difference is to let there be a monetary reform in the current year which changes all prices in the same proportion. It is with reference to such a monetary reform that van Yzeren (1958) sought to demonstrate the failure of the new index numbers to satisfy the comparative proportionality test (which he confusingly described as 'the so-called proportionality test', thus creating the erroneous impression that his test, which he formulated correctly, was the same as Fisher's). In order to make his point he argued as follows (P stands for P_S and Q for Q_S): 'Suppose that just before the reform $V = 0.90$, $P_L = 1.24$, $Q_L = 0.79$. These data give $P = 1.20$, $Q = 0.75$. Immediately after the reform all prices are halved, so $V = 0.45$, $P_L = 0.62$, $Q_L = 0.79$. Now we find $P = 0.59$, $Q = 0.76$. Clearly some bias has crept in.' On the face of it this appears to be a pretty conclusive argument. However, as soon as it is realised that the currency units in which the prices are measured before and after the monetary reform cannot be the same, even if they carry the same name, it becomes clear that van Yzeren's argument is seriously flawed, because the second part of his argument ignores the unit change that has been brought about by the monetary reform. In order to make a proper comparison between prices in the current year and prices in the base year, both will have to be measured either in pre-reform units or in post-reform units, just as in comparisons between US and UK prices we have to express both sets of prices either in dollars or in pounds sterling (compare section 6.1).

The second way of bringing the comparative proportionality test into play is by comparing two different current years with a given base year, but even then it is only relevant on condition that the prices in the one current year are k times the corresponding prices in the other. Of course, the fact that the comparative proportionality test in this context is no more than a conditional test tends to reduce its importance. However, we should not forget that the failure of the Fisher index numbers to meet such a conditional test, namely the withdrawal-and-entry test, proved to be more serious than it appeared at first sight, since it was bound up with the failure of those index numbers to meet the more general aggregation test, a test which was not known to Fisher (see section 4.20). Therefore, if the failure of the new index numbers to meet the comparative proportionality test were likewise indicative of their failure to meet an as yet unknown more general test, it might be a serious matter. But, unless and until such a more general test is shown to exist, there is in my view little or nothing in the comparative proportionality test to detract from the analytically desirable properties of the new index numbers.

Von Bortkiewicz Formulae

No doubt one of the most remarkable achievements in index-number theory is the linking of the relative gap between the Laspeyres and Paasche volume and price index numbers for a commodity aggregate, with the correlation between the quantity and price relatives of the single commodities comprised in that aggregate. As is so often the case with remarkable achievements, the underlying idea of this particular one, which is due to von Bortkiewicz (1923), is extraordinarily simple. The essential link between the index-number gap and the correlation between price and quantity relatives is the weighted covariance of the latter. Quite generally, the covariance of two associated variables x and y is defined as the mean-cross-product of the associated values of those variables measured in deviation from their means $\bar{x}$ and $\bar{y}$. But in case each pair of associated values of the variables x and y is assigned a weight w^i the covariance of x and y should be weighted as well. As such it becomes

$$\mathrm{Cov}_w(x, y) = \frac{\Sigma w^i(x^i-\bar{x})\,(y^i-\bar{y})}{\Sigma w^i}$$

$$= \frac{\Sigma w^ix^iy^i - \bar{x}\Sigma w^iy^i - \bar{y}\Sigma w^ix^i + \bar{x}\bar{y}\Sigma w^i}{\Sigma w^i}$$

$$= \frac{\Sigma w^ix^iy^i}{\Sigma w^i} - \frac{\Sigma w^ix^i}{\Sigma w^i} \cdot \frac{\Sigma w^iy^i}{\Sigma w^i}$$

since $\bar{x} = \dfrac{\Sigma w^ix^i}{\Sigma w^i}$ and $\bar{y} = \dfrac{\Sigma w^iy^i}{\Sigma w^i}$

(i) Putting $x^i = Q_1^i/Q_0^i$, $y^i = P_1^i/P_0^i$ and $w^i = Q_0^iP_0^i$, so that $\bar{x} = Q_L$ and $\bar{y} = P_L$, this translates into

$$\mathrm{Cov}_{w_0}(q, p) = \Sigma w_0^i(q^i-Q_L)\,(p^i-P_L) = V - Q_LP_L$$

where $q^i = Q_1^i/Q_0^i$, $p^i = P_1^i/P_0^i$ and $w_0^i = Q_0^iP_0^i/\Sigma Q_0^ip_0^i$

Since, by virtue of the double identity $V \equiv Q_LP_P \equiv Q_PP_L$, we can write

$$V - Q_LP_L = Q_L(P_P-P_L) = P_L(Q_P-Q_L)$$

107

it follows that

$$\text{Cov}_{w_0}(q, p) = Q_L(P_P - P_L) = P_L(Q_P - Q_L)$$

With the help of this expression for the base-weighted covariance of the quantity and price relatives, the expression for the gap coefficient (g) in (1.19) becomes practically self-explanatory, given the definition of the correlation coefficient as the ratio between the covariance and the product of the standard deviations of the associated variables.

(ii) Likewise, by putting $x^i = Q_2^i/Q_1^i$, $y^i = P_0^i/P_1^i$ and $w^i = Q_1^i P_1^i$, so that $\bar{x} = Q_L^{12}$ and $\bar{y} = P_L^{10}$, we find the expression for the covariance in (5.26) to be

$$\text{Cov}_{w_1}(q^{12}, p^{10}) = Q_L^{12,\,0} P_L^{10} - Q_L^{12} P_L^{10}$$

since $\Sigma Q_2^i P_0^i / \Sigma Q_1^i P_1^i = Q_L^{12,\,0} P_L^{10}$

(iii) Finally, by putting $x^i = Q_2^i/Q_1^i$, $y^i = P_1^i/P_0^i$ and $w^i = Q_1^i P_0^i$, so that $\bar{x} = Q_L^{12,0}$ and $\bar{y} = P_P^{01}$, we find the expression for the covariance in (5.40) to be

$$\text{Cov}_{w_{10}}(q^{12}, p^{01}) = Q_L^{12} P_P^{01} - Q_L^{12,\,0} P_P^{01}$$

since $\Sigma Q_2^i P_1^i / \Sigma Q_1^i P_0^i = Q_L^{12} P_P^{01}$

The Relation Between P_S and P_F

Törnqvist (1958) pointed out in a comment on the new index numbers that, while they have the property

$$P_L - Q_L = P_S - Q_S, \quad P_S Q_S = V$$

the Fisher index numbers have the property

$$P_L/Q_L = P_F/Q_F, \quad P_F Q_F = V$$

This interesting observation led him to suspect that in practice P_S will be almost equal to P_F. In order to verify that this indeed would normally be the case, he developed a formula for the difference between P_S and P_F. This formula should have been

$$P_S - P_F = \frac{(P_L - Q_L)(P_F - P_P)}{(P_S + Q_L) - (P_L - P_F)}$$

but inadvertently he replaced the $(P_F - P_P)$ in the numerator by $(P_L - P_F)$. Using his formula he found that $P_S - P_F = 0.0053$ for $P_L - P_F = 0.1$, $P_L - Q_L = 0.1$ and $P_S + Q_L = 2$. (The correct formula gives the same result for $P_F - P_P = 0.1$, $P_L - Q_L = 0.1$ and $(P_S + Q_L) - (P_L + P_F) = Q_S + P_F = 1.9$.) On the basis of this finding Törnqvist concluded: 'A difference of the order of size of 10 per cent between the price index of Laspeyres and Fisher occurs only in rare practical cases. Stuvel's index will thus rarely differ from Fisher's ideal index by an amount large enough to be seen in the figures used for presenting the results.'

Apart from the flaw in his formula for $P_S - P_F$, the main weakness in Törnqvist's argument lies in his putting $P_L - Q_L = 0.1$. By doing so he simply assumed away the main cause of differences between P_S and P_F. There are in fact many instances in which the difference between P_L and Q_L, and thus that between P_S and P_F, is much larger. Examples can be found in comparisons over long periods, particularly if a war has intervened, in comparisons between countries and in short-run comparisons when the situation is one of hyperinflation or one of adjustment to the effects of a currency devaluation or rapidly changing terms of trade.

109

In order to express the difference between P_S and P_F in an analytically meaningful manner, it is worth noting that, according to the correct formula for $P_S - P_F$ shown above, $P_S = P_F$ either if $P_F = P_P$, i.e. $P_P = P_L$, or if $P_L = Q_L$. Expressed in relative terms the first of these two cases arises if $g = 0$ and the second if $h = h' = 1$, where $g = \dfrac{P_P - P_L}{P_L} = \dfrac{Q_P - Q_L}{Q_L}$ (see section

1.14) and where $h = \dfrac{1}{h'} = \dfrac{Q_L}{P_L}$. From these expressions for g and h it

follows directly that $P_P = (1 + g)P_L$ and $Q_L = hP_L$. Hence, since $V = Q_L P_P = Q_P P_L$, $V = h(1 + g)P_L^2$ and $Q_P = h(1 + g)P_L$. Therefore

$$P_S = \tfrac{1}{2}P_L[(1-h) + \sqrt{(1-h)^2 + 4h(1+g)}]$$

and

$$P_F = P_L\sqrt{1+g}$$

Consequently

$$P_S - P_F = P_L\left[\frac{(1-h) + \sqrt{(1-h)^2 + 4h(1+g)}}{2} - \sqrt{1+g}\right]$$

Not surprisingly the absolute difference between P_S and P_F is seen to depend not only on g and h, but also on P_L. The relative difference $(P_S - P_F)/P_L$, however, is only dependent on g and h. And so is the ratio which compares the gap between P_S and P_F with the gap between P_L and P_P:

$$\frac{P_S - P_F}{P_L - P_P} = \frac{1}{g}\left[\sqrt{(1+g)} - \frac{(1-h) + \sqrt{(1-h)^2 + 4h(1+g)}}{2}\right]$$

Likewise we find

$$\frac{Q_S - Q_F}{Q_L - Q_P} = \frac{1}{g}\left[\sqrt{(1+g)} - \frac{(1-h') + \sqrt{(1-h')^2 \, 4h'(1+g)}}{2}\right]$$

The table opposite shows the numerical value of these two gap ratios for a number of combinations of g-values and of h or h'-values. The latter are chosen in such a way that a direct comparison can be made between the numerical values of the $(P_S - P_F)/(P_L - P_P)$ price-gap ratio and the corresponding $(Q_S - Q_F)/(Q_L - Q_P)$ quantity-gap ratio. Thus, for instance, the price-gap ratio for $g = -0.3$ and $h = 2$ is -0.17 and the corresponding quantity-gap ratio for $g = -0.3$ and $h = 2$, i.e. $h' = 1/h = 0.5$, is 0.19. This possibility of direct comparison has been achieved by the simple device of making the h-values to the left of the central column the reciprocals of those to the right of it, and vice versa.

Numerical values of $(P_S - P_F)/(P_L - P_P)$ and $(Q_S - Q_F)/(Q_L - Q_P)$
for selected values of g, h, and h'*

h or h' =	0.25	0.5	0.8	1	1.25	2	4
g = −0.5	0.37	0.20	0.07	0	−0.06	−0.18	−0.29
−0.3	0.33	0.19	0.06	0	−0.06	−0.17	−0.30
−0.1	0.31	0.17	0.06	0	−0.06	−0.17	−0.30
0							
0.1	0.29	0.16	0.05	0	−0.05	−0.16	−0.30
0.3	0.28	0.15	0.05	0	−0.05	−0.16	−0.30
0.5	0.26	0.15	0.05	0	−0.05	−0.16	−0.30

* $g = (Q_P - Q_L)/Q_L = (P_P - P_L)/P_L$; $h = Q_L/P_L$; $h' = P_L/Q_L$.

A number of interesting points emerge from this table. We note in particular the following:

(a) There is near symmetry, though not complete symmetry, between the columns on either side of the central column, apart from the difference in sign. That is to say, for given g and h the price-gap ratio and the corresponding quantity-gap ratio have numerical values that are roughly equal, apart from having opposite signs.

(b) Row-wise there is far less difference than column-wise; in fact there is hardly any difference at all row-wise, except for very low h or h'-values. This suggests that the gap coefficient (g) affects these gap ratios only slightly, their main determinant being the ratio between the Laspeyres quantity and price indexes (i.e. either h or h').

(c) Most important of all, when the index-number problem is acute in the sense that the numerical difference between the Laspeyres index and the corresponding Paasche index is such that it cannot be ignored, the numerical difference between the corresponding new index and Fisher index, although smaller, may be far from negligible, particularly if h differs considerably from unity, i.e. if the price development of the aggregate (as measured by P_L) is very much stronger or weaker than its quantity development (as measured by Q_L).

Notes and References

References are to author and year of publication of article or book, e.g. Allen (1975). The full titles are given in the Bibliography.

1 The Problem

1. These matters are dealt with at length in Allen (1975) and Stone (1956).
2. See Irving Fisher (1927) p.3.
3. See Irving Fisher (1927) pp.489 and 490.
4. See Fowler (1970) p.4.
5. For a brief discussion of the analytical significance of the sign of the gap coefficient see Stuvel (1986) pp.54–5.

2 The Traditional Approach

1. See Edgeworth (1925) p.213.
2. See Irving Fisher (1927) p.396.

3 The Analytical Approach

1. Compare Gorman (1986).
2. See Stuvel (1957).

4 Properties and Tests

1. See Montgomery (1937) p.65.
2. See van Yzeren (1958) p.434.
3. These tests are discussed in Appendix I of Irving Fisher (1927) pp.420–6.
4. See Irving Fisher (1927) p.420.
5. The statement by Siegel (1965) that P_s does not satisfy Fisher's proportionality test and does no better at meeting the identity test is clearly wide of the mark.
6. See Irving Fisher (1927) p.420.
7. Ibid. p.420.
8. Ibid. pp.423–6.
9. Ibid. p.420.

5 Indirect and Chain Indices

1. See Westergaard (1890) p.219.

112

6 Other Transitive Indices

1. See Gini (1931) p.9/10.
2. See Geary (1958).
3. See Irving Fisher (1927) p.485.
4. See van Yzeren (1957).
5. The ratios in this table are all of the type P_Y^{ts}/P_D^{ts} where $t = A$ and $s = A$, B, C, D. Note that $P_L^{st} = 1/P_P^{ts}$, so that the relevant ratios for the van Yzeren method I price indices are $P_L(\mathrm{I})/P_P$ and $P_P(\mathrm{I})/P_L$. Likewise $Q_L(\mathrm{I})/Q_P$ and $Q_P(\mathrm{I})/Q_L$ are the relevant ratios for the van Yzeren method I volume indices.

Irving Fisher's Search for the Ideal Index Number

1. See Irving Fisher (1927) p.219.

Banerjee's Factorial Index Numbers

1. See Banerjee (1975) pp.102–5 and Banerjee (1987) pp.5–13.
2. See Banerjee (1987) p.13.
3. See R.A. Fisher (1966).

Bibliography

Allen, R.G.D. (1975) *Index Numbers in Theory and Practice* (London).

Banerjee, K.S. (1975) *Cost of Living Index Numbers* (New York).

Banerjee, K.S. (1987) *On the Factorial Approach to Index Number Problems, Consumption Analysis and Orthogonal Decomposition of National Income: A Summary* (College Park).

Bortkiewicz, L. von (1923) 'Zweck und Struktur einer Preisindexzahl, Erster Artikel' in *Nordisk Statistisk Tidskrift*, pp. 369–408.

Edgeworth, F.Y. (1925) *Papers Relating to Political Economy*, (London), vol. I, pp. 198–259, reprinted from *Report of the 57th Meeting of the British Association for the Advancement of Science* (London, 1888).

Fisher, Irving (1927) *The Making of Index Numbers*, 3rd edn (Boston): 1st edn 1922.

Fisher, R.A. (1966) *The Design of Experiments*, 8th edn (Edinburgh).

Fowler, R.F. (1970) *Some Problems of Index Number Construction*, CSO Studies in Official Statistics, Research Series no. 3 (London).

Geary, R.C. (1958) 'A Note on the Comparison of Exchange Rates and Purchasing Power between Countries', *Journal of the Royal Statistical Society*, Series A, pp. 97–9.

Gini, C. (1931) 'On the Circular Test of Index Numbers', *Metron*, pp. 3–24.

Gorman, W.M. (1986) 'Compatible Indices', *The Economic Journal*, Conference Papers Supplement, pp. 83–95.

Laspeyres, E. (1871) 'Die Berechnung einer mittleren Waarenpreissteigerung', *Jahrbücher für Nationalökonomie und Statistik*, pp. 296–314.

Montgomery, J.K. (1937) *The Mathematical Problem of the Price Index* (London).

Paasche, H. (1874) 'Ueber die Preisentwicklung der letzten Jahre nach den Hamburger Börsennotirungen', *Jahrbücher für Nationalökonomie und Statistik*, pp. 168–78.

Siegel, Irving H. (1965) 'Systems of Algebraically Consistent Index Numbers', *Proceedings of the Business and Statistics Section of the American Statistical Association* (Washington, DC) pp. 369–72.

Stone, J.R.N. (1956) *Quantity and Price Indexes in National Accounts* (Paris).

Stuvel, G. (1957) 'A New Index Number Formula', *Econometrica*, pp. 123–31.

Stuvel, G. (1986) *National Accounts Analysis* (London).

Törnqvist, L. (1958) Review of Stuvel (1957) in *Mathematical Reviews*, p. 371–2.

Vartia, Y.O. (1976) 'Ideal Log-change Index Numbers', *Scandinavian Journal of Statistics*, pp. 121–6.

Westergaard, H. (1890) *Die Grundzüge der Statistik* (Jena).

Yzeren, J. van (1957) *Three Methods of Comparing the Purchasing Power of Currencies*, The Netherlands Central Bureau of Statistics, Statistical Studies No. 7, (Zeist).

Yzeren, J. van (1958) 'A Note on the Useful Properties of Stuvel's Index Numbers', *Econometrica*, pp. 429–39.

Index